AMERI CUTTING EDGE

LEVEL 4

PEARSON
Longman

The English Language Training College

WORKBOOK

jane comyns carr   frances eales

Contents

Introduction

Grammar terms

1 Look at these grammar terms and match them with one of the underlined words from the jokes above.

a a countable noun *lies*

b an uncountable noun ....

c an adjective ....

d a preposition ....

e an adverb ....

f the base form of the verb ....

g the *-ing* form of the verb ....

h an auxiliary verb ....

i a modal auxiliary verb ....

j a definite article ....

k an indefinite article ....

l a pronoun ....

m a possessive adjective ....

n a conjunction ....

Using a dictionary

2 A dictionary can be very useful to find the grammar of a word. Look at these two extracts from the *Longman Active Study Dictionary* and complete the sentences below.

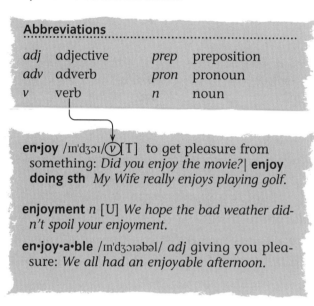

> **Abbreviations** ....
>
> | | | | |
> |---|---|---|---|
> | *adj* | adjective | *prep* | preposition |
> | *adv* | adverb | *pron* | pronoun |
> | *v* | verb | *n* | noun |

> **en·joy** /ɪnˈdʒɔɪ/ ⓥ [T] to get pleasure from something: *Did you enjoy the movie?*| **enjoy doing sth** *My Wife really enjoys playing golf.*
>
> **enjoyment** *n* [U] *We hope the bad weather didn't spoil your enjoyment.*
>
> **en·joy·a·ble** /ɪnˈdʒɔɪəbəl/ *adj* giving you pleasure: *We all had an enjoyable afternoon.*

> **train²** /treɪn/ *v* [T] to teach someone how to do something, especially the practical skills they need to do a job: *Staff are trained in how to deal with difficult customers.*
>
> **train·ee** /ˌtreɪˈniː/ *n* [C] someone who is being trained for a job: *a trainee teacher*
>
> **train·er** /ˈtreɪnər/ *n* [C] someone whose job is to train people how to do something
>
> **train·ing** /ˈtreɪnɪŋ/ *n* [U] when someone is taught the skills they need to do something: *a training course*

a   enjoy is ..*a verb*..........

b   enjoyment is ....

c   enjoyable is ....

d   train is ....

e   trainee is ....

f   trainer is ....

g   training is ....

3 Complete each sentence with one of the words from exercise 2.

a   Where did Jenny ..*train*.......................... to be a ski instructor?

b   My father gets a lot of .... from his yard.

c   I really .... spending time on my own.

d   How much soccer .... do you do every day?

e   The course was really .... I recommend it.

f   Patricia's only a .... chef, but her cooking is fantastic!

g   Our .... wants us to finish our project this week.

module 1

Making questions

1 Use the prompts to write complete questions in the following situations.

a) Steve is asking Phil about his new girlfriend, Cinzia, who comes from Italy.

1 What / be / her name?
   What's her name ....?

2 Which part of Italy / she / come from?
   ....?

3 How / you / meet / her?
   ....?

4 What / she / do for a living?
   ....?

5 When / she first / come / to England?
   ....?

6 How well / she / speak English?
   ....?

7 she / like / London?
   ....?

8 she / have / an apartment here?
   ....?

b) Sarah wants to emigrate to Australia with her family. An official is asking her some questions.

1 When / you / get married?
   ....?

2 Where / your husband / born?
   ....?

3 your husband / work?
   ....?

4 he / have / any qualifications?
   ....?

5 How many children / you / have?
   ....?

6 How old / be / your children?
   ....?

7 you / know / anybody in Australia?
   ....?

Short answers

- *Do you like rock music?* | Yes, I like rock music. **Yes, I do.**

- *Did you enjoy the movie?* | No, I didn't enjoy the movie. **No, I didn't.**

The long answer is unnatural, so we use a short answer.

2 Look at these long answers. First write the questions and then write a short answer for each one.

a No, I'm not married.
   Are you married ....?
   No, I'm not ....

b Yes, I live with my family.
   ....?
   ....

c No, we don't live in an apartment.
   ....?
   ....

d No, we didn't live in the same place when I was young.
   ....
   ....?
   ....

e No, my grandparents aren't alive.
   ....?
   ....

f No, I don't have a car.
   ....?
   ....

g Yes, I can understand English well.
   ....?
   ....

h No, my English teacher doesn't speak my language.
   ....?
   ....

Question tags

> **LOOK!**
>
> • **He has** her phone number, **doesn't he**?
>   **+**   **−**
> • **It isn't** very warm today, **is it**?
>   **−**   **+**
>
> Notice:
> 1 **You take** sugar in your coffee, **don't you**?
>   ↑ no auxiliary   ↑ auxiliary **do**
> 2 **I'm really early, aren't I**?
>   ~~amn't I~~?

3 **a)** Complete these sentences with a question tag.

1) Two friends are shopping:

a   Ooh, it's cold today, _isn't it_ ?

b   That coat costs a lot, ...?

c   They have some nice clothes here, ...?

d   These jeans are too short, ...?

e   There aren't many sales clerks here, ...?

2) Mrs. Halliday is talking to Liesbeth, who has come to stay for six months and help with the children:

a   You're from Amsterdam, ...?

b   You speak French, ...?

c   You have two little brothers, ...?

d   You don't smoke, ...?

e   You can drive, ...?

b) 📼 Listen to the statements and add the correct question tag.

You hear: **You say:**

Ooh, it's cold today, ...   _Ooh, it's cold today, isn't it?_

Present Simple or Continuous

4 Mike, a salesman, is talking to his doctor about his stress problems. Complete the sentences with the best form of the verb in parentheses.

DOCTOR: How can I help you, Mr. Daniels?

MIKE: Well, I started having bad headaches a couple of weeks ago and they (1) _'re / are getting_ (get) worse. I can't sleep properly, I'm tired all the time, and the worst thing is my hair (2) .... (go) gray and I'm only 31!

DOCTOR: I see. Let me ask you some questions. (3) .... (you / smoke)?

MIKE: No, I gave up a month ago.

DOCTOR: Right. I see you're a salesman. On average how many hours a week (4) .... (you / work)?

MIKE: Well, I normally (5) .... (do) eight hours a day, but at the moment I (6) .... (work) at least ten hours and some Saturdays.

DOCTOR: That is a lot. And so how (7) .... (you / relax)?

MIKE: Well, I usually (8) .... (sit) in front of the TV with a pizza and a few beers.

DOCTOR: Hmm. (9) .... (you / do) any exercise at the moment?

MIKE: Not really, but I'm losing a lot of weight and I (10) .... (not / know) why.

DOCTOR: I think you (11) .... (suffer) from stress. I (12) .... (want) you to eat a more varied diet and to do some exercise. Come back and see me in four weeks and I'll check you again.

State or action verbs

5 The following conversation takes place in a camera store. Complete the sentences with the best form of the verb in parentheses.

A: Good morning, how can I help?

B: Well, I (1) *'m looking* .... (*look for*) a compact camera with a 200 m lens.

A: Right. Well, this new model's very good. It (2) .... (*have*) a zoom and a built-in flash and it only (3) .... (*cost*) £150.

B: Ah. You see I (4) .... (*buy*) it for a friend and he (5) .... (*not / want*) to spend more than £100.

A: OK, I (6) .... (*understand*) the problem. Let's see – I (7) .... (*think*) the Zenco 460 is a very good buy. There's a picture here in the catalog.

B: Oh, yes, that (8) .... (*look*) nice.

A: The only problem is that we (9) .... (*not have*) any in the store at the moment. In fact, we (10) .... (*wait*) for some to come from our other store in Oxford.

B: Right, so when will they be here?

A: Well, I (11) .... (*not know*) exactly. I really need to ask the manager, but I'm afraid she (12) .... (*have*) lunch at the moment. She'll be back in about half an hour.

B: OK. Perhaps I'll come back later.

Word order
Adverbs of frequency

Some adverbs come before the main verb, but after the verb *to be*:

I	always nearly always	do my homework.
I'm	quite often sometimes occasionally hardly ever never	late for class.

Some adverbs go at the beginning **or** end of the sentence:

Most of the time	I do my homework	most of the time.
Sometimes Occasionally	I'm late for class	sometimes. occasionally.

6 a) Rewrite these sentences with the adverb in the correct position (there may be more than one correct answer).

1 I speak English on the phone. (*sometimes*)
I sometimes speak English on the phone ....

2 My colleague Jo uses my computer. (*occasionally*)
....

3 My classmate Carla has lunch with me. (*quite often*)
....
....

4 My boss is in the office. (*hardly ever*)
....

5 My neighbors are very quiet. (*most of the time*)
....
....

6 My sister-in-law Jenny phones me on Mondays. (*nearly always*)
....
....

7 Paul's relatives visit us at Christmas. (*always*)
....

8 Stephen sees his ex-girlfriend. (*hardly ever*)
....

9 Daryl, my roommate, cleans the bathroom. (*never*)
....
....

b) Write five sentences in your notebook about how often you do things. Show them to your teacher.

Pronunciation

/ə/ (schwa)

> **LOOK!**
>
> • *husband* has 2 syllables: husband
>   ●   ○
>   /ə/
>
> • *acquaintance* has 3 syllables: acquaintance
>   ○   ●   ○
>   /ə/   /ə/
>
> In *husband* "hus" is stressed (it is stronger and longer) and "band" is unstressed (it is weaker and shorter). In *acquaintance* the second syllable is stressed and the first and third syllables are unstressed.
>
> We often pronounce the unstressed syllable /ə/.

7 a) Notice where the stress falls in the words below. Which sounds are pronounced /ə/? Write the symbol underneath.

1 economy
   /ə/

2 stepmother

3 couple

4 brother-in-law

5 photograph

6 stranger

7 relative

8 foreign

9 principal

10 neighbor

11 partner

12 parent

b) Listen and repeat the words, paying attention to the stress and /ə/ sound.

c) Listen and mark the stress and /ə/ sound(s) on the following words.

1 often
   /ə/

2 occasionally

3 usually

4 assistant

5 salesman

6 catalog

The letter *s*

> **LOOK!**
>
> The letter *s* can be pronounced /s/, /z/, or /ɪz/ in:
> • plural forms of nouns:
>   *roommates, neighbors, marriages*
>   /s/   /z/   /ɪz/
> • Present Simple, third person singular:
>   *she smokes, he learns, it increases*
>   /s/   /z/   /ɪz/

8 a) Listen to the nouns and verbs in the box (or say them aloud) and complete the chart below.

> ~~wants~~ nieces spells entertains practices parents acquaintances relatives uses classmates colleagues hopes works spends pronounces

/s/	/z/	/ɪz/
wants		

b) Listen again and repeat the words.

Grammar snack

both / neither

9 **a)** Carl is studying English in Edinburgh. His friend Julie is studying Psychology at Bath University. Read these extracts from their letters to each other and decide which of the statements below are correct.

Julie

... I'm really enjoying the course, although I have a lot of work to do in the evening, apart from Fridays and Saturdays, when I go dancing or to a bar. I'm glad that I came to Bath University – the city is really beautiful. The university is on a hill just outside the city, and there is a bus service, but I usually cycle, which takes about an hour. Actually, I'm getting quite fit, because I go jogging most mornings. How are you getting along in ...

Carl

... and my teacher gives us homework nearly every day, so I spend at least an hour doing that in the evening, before I go out. I usually go to a bar – the bars here in Edinburgh are always busy and the people are really friendly. I met a Scottish boy in a bar soon after I arrived and – guess what – we go fishing together every Sunday. My only problem now is that I have a long journey by bus to school every morning. I think I'll start looking for new accommodations nearer to school ...

1 a They both have a lot of work to do. ✔
   b Carl has a lot of work, but Julie doesn't.

2 a Julie is doing a lot of exercise, but Carl isn't.
   b They are both doing a lot of exercise.

3 a Neither of them go dancing at weekends.
   b Julie goes dancing at weekends, and Carl goes fishing.

4 a Neither of them go to bars.
   b Both of them go to bars.

5 a Neither Carl nor Julie live near their school / university.
   b Both Carl and Julie live near their school / university.

b) Correct these sentences.

1 My ex-girlfriend and I (liked) both traveling.

2 Neither my neighbors are noisy.

3 Both my sister and my niece spends a lot of time cooking.

4 My colleagues Dan and Rob are quite lazy: neither of them doesn't do much work.

5 My best friend June and I both are learning a musical instrument.

6 Neither Ann and Susan likes watching soccer.

c) Write five sentences about your friends / colleagues / classmates / family with *both* and *neither*.

1 ....
....

2 ....
....

3 ....
....

4 ....
....

5 ....
....

LOOK!

Notice the position of *both* in these examples:

• They **both** have a lot of homework.

• They are **both** students.

• **Both** of them are studying.

Notice the forms we can use with *neither*:

• **Neither** of them work / works.

• **Neither** Carl **nor** Julie live / lives ...

• **Neither** Carl **nor** Julie ~~doesn't~~ live / lives ...

Vocabulary

Activities with *do* / *play* / *go*

10 **a)** Put the activities in the box into the correct column in the chart below (six for each verb). Mark the stress on each word.

> the drums   sports   photography   ~~cycling~~   swimming   gardening
> the guitar   cards   knitting   exercise   snooker   a computer game
> yoga   jogging   skiing   dancing   volleyball   walking

do	play	go
		• cycling

b) 🖵 Listen to the prompts and say the correct verb.

You hear:
... the drums

You say:
play the drums

> • We use **play** for musical instruments and games with rules.
> • We use **go** for hobbies and sports, especially when we have to go somewhere to do them (with expressions such as *a lot of, a bit of, some / any* we can use *do*: "I do a lot of walking").
> • We use **do** for other hobbies (often creative hobbies).

c) Match these questions and answers and complete the sentences with the correct form of *do*, *play*, or *go*.

1   That's a lovely sweater. Where did you get it?

2   Where are the children? They're very quiet.

3   Do you .... a lot of exercise?

4   Would you like to .... dancing?

5   How did you learn to .... the drums?

6   Do you know much about cameras?

a   I think they're .... a computer game.

b   No, but ask John; he .... a lot of photography.

c   I taught myself.

d   Not really – but I .... swimming occasionally.

e   Oh, my grandmother made it. She *does*........ a lot of knitting.

f   I'd love to. When?

1 ...*e*...   2 ....   3 ....   4 ....   5 ....   6 ....

Improve your writing

Spelling of the *-ing* form

> **LOOK!**
>
> To make the *-ing* form, we usually add *-ing* to the base form of the verb: *sleeping, reading, opening*.
>
> There are three exceptions:
>
> • One-syllable verbs, e.g. *put*, where there is a single vowel *u* and then a consonant *t*, we double the final consonant: *putting*. (We never double *x*, *y*, or *w*: *boxing, buying, knowing*.)
>
> • Verbs that end in a single *-e*, lose the *-e*: *make – making*.
>
> • These three verbs (with two syllables) double the final consonant: *forget – forgetting, begin – beginning, occur – occurring*.

11 Spell the *-ing* form of these verbs.

a   read *reading*........

b   pay ....

c   write ....

d   see ....

e   begin ....

f   fax ....

g   hope ....

h   plan ....

i   jog ....

j   forget ....

k   print ....

l   answer ....

m   train ....

n   grow ....

o   drive ....

Listen and read
Unusual lifestyles

12 **a)** 📼 Three people are talking about their lifestyles. Read and / or listen to the texts. What are their jobs?

Gemma

"I absolutely love music and listen to it all the time, even when I go jogging. Of course I have to look after my voice. I do exercises for three hours every day and I take lots of vitamin C. If I get a sore throat I go straight to bed and rest. I usually try to get at least eight hours' sleep a night anyway. ... As for my job – you really can't be shy in this kind of work, and you have to be very patient because sometimes we practice for hours before we get it right. When we're on tour, we work for several weeks with no breaks and you can get really tired. For relaxation, whenever I get a vacation, I go straight to a sunny beach, but the thing I enjoy the most is the great feeling you get from a live audience."

1 Gemma is a / an

....

2 Raoul is a / an

....

3 Frank is a / an

....

Raoul

"Well, my work's really quite stressful. Most people think you spend your day chopping vegetables and stirring soup, but it's not that simple. You have to be really careful with the food and keep everything very clean. The big problem is my boss — he shouts at me all the time — even, for example, if I forget to wash one plate — I just can't do anything right sometimes. Actually, I'm hoping to find a new job soon because I don't get much time off. I'd like to have more weekends free, to see friends and to spend more time with my two little boys. You know it's strange spending all day with food — when I go home I just want to eat a sandwich or French fries and I'm terribly critical when I eat in a restaurant."

Frank

"Well, I first got interested because I loved doing them so much myself — I used to do at least one every day. I suppose I have the right kind of mind really — I enjoy playing around with puzzles, especially word puzzles. So I sent a couple in to a local newspaper and was really surprised when they asked me for more. I suppose it is a strange way to spend your day — surrounded by dictionaries and

books, but it's great that I can organize my own time, so I try to finish by two and then I can take my dog for a walk. It's very satisfying though — I love the feeling after I've thought of the final clue, and it all fits together. It's also really nice when people write to me and thank me. Funny really, because I'm just doing what I like."

b) Read and / or listen again, and answer these questions:

Who:

1 works with food? *Raoul*.........

2 isn't happy in their job? ....

3 spends a lot of time reading? ....

4 is careful about their health? ....

5 has a logical mind? ....

6 likes being in front of lots of people? ....

7 has two sons? ....

8 has free afternoons? ....

9 practices a lot? ....

10 has a very strict boss? ....

module 2

Past Simple or Continuous

1 Choose a phrase from each box to make a complete answer for the questions below.

I was peeling some onions and
She was traveling home from work and she
We were sunbathing on the weekend and we
They were staying in Florida when
He was walking in the rain and he
He was playing soccer and he

got very wet.
stayed out too long.
the knife slipped.
left it on the bus.
fell over.
there was a terrible storm.

a How did you cut your finger?
I was peeling some onions and the knife slipped .

b How did Tony hurt his knee?
....

c How did you all get so sunburned?
....

d How did Martin catch a cold?
....

e How did a tree fall on the Simpsons' car?
....

f How did Sara lose her purse?
....

2 Complete these dialogs with the best form of the verb in parentheses.

A: I phoned you last night at 8:00 but you didn't answer. What (1) *were you doing*............. (you do)?

B: I (2) .... (work) on my computer and I (3) ....(not hear) the phone ring. Sorry!

A: Good morning. International Chemicals Incorporated. May I help you?

B: Hello, yes I (4) .... (talk) to the Financial Director a minute ago and the line (5) .... (go) dead.

A: Oh, I'm sorry, Madam. I'll reconnect you.

A: When did you meet your husband?

B: When I (6) .... (be) in Canada last winter.

A: Were you on vacation?

B: No, I (7) .... (train) to be a ski instructor, but on the second day I (8) .... (break) my leg. I (9) .... (spend) eight weeks in hospital and he was my doctor!

3 Use the prompts to write two conversations about accidents. Choose the best form of the verb.

a A: Penny told me you / have / accident yesterday. What / happen ?
Penny told me you had an accident yesterday.
What happened ?

B: We / drive / home and another car / stop / suddenly and we / crash / into it.
....
....
....

A: Be / the other car all right?
.... ?

B: Yes, luckily we / not / go / very fast.
....
....

b A: How / your brother get that scar /
   his hand?

   ....

   ....

   ....?

   B: He / get / it / while we / live / in
   Italy.

   ....

   ....

   ....

   A: Oh, how?

   B: He / play / near the oven and he /
   burn / his hand on the oven door.

   ....

   ....

   ....

   A: Ooh, nasty!

Pronunciation

Syllable stress in Past Simple forms

4 **a)** How many syllables do these
-ed forms have? Mark the stressed
syllables ● and the unstressed
syllables ○.

     ● ○
1 happened   9 practiced

     ●
2 stopped   10 decided

3 traveled   11 improved

4 looked   12 received

5 reminded   13 repeated

6 watched   14 started

7 asked   15 closed

8 changed

b) 🔲 Listen to the verbs in phrases
and repeat them.

used to

5 Read the text and mark the sentences below *T* (true) or *F* (false).
Underline the words in the text that help you decide.

Recently a Russian friend came to visit me. It was one of her lifelong dreams to visit London, and she certainly knows more about the city than I do. She arrived at lunchtime and we spent a tiring afternoon going around the Tower of London. However, by five o'clock I couldn't help noticing that she didn't seem as enthusiastic as she had been earlier. I asked if anything was wrong and she said, "This is all very interesting but where is the fog and where are the men in bowler hats? Why did everyone push to get on the bus at the bus stop instead of standing in line? It's very different from the books I've read about England."

Her comments made me think. It's true that people don't stand in line much anymore: nowadays you often find that everyone just jumps on the bus. Or maybe this is only in London. Also the idea of a man standing up and offering his seat to a woman on a train or bus is unusual these days, although my father still does it!

As for the weather: well, we all know that a hundred years ago there used to be fog in London throughout the year, but we no longer have much fog; nowadays we have pollution from all the cars! Over the last few years in the summer London has been one of the hottest places in Europe, although we still get more than enough rain in the other seasons.

What about the city men in their working "uniform"? Well, you can still see some city "gents" in their smart suits, but men hardly ever wear bowler hats. A few things don't change, though. If you try to start a conversation with an English person on the subway in London, she or he will probably look at you as if you are crazy!

a Everything was as she expected it to be. ..F..

b People don't stand in line as much as they used to. .....

c Men used to give up their seats to women on public
   transportation. .....

d It still rains a lot in winter. .....

e Most London businessmen no longer wear bowler hats. .....

f People used to talk to each other on trains and still do. .....

6 Linda's life has changed a lot in the past ten years. Write six sentences about the changes using *used to* and *didn't use to* (the words in parentheses will help you).

LINDA TEN YEARS AGO

LINDA NOW

a (smoke) *She used to smoke* .

b (hair) ....

c (car) ....

d (boyfriend) ....

e (smart clothes) ....

f (unhappy) ....

still, not anymore / any longer

LOOK!

When we use *still, not anymore / any longer* in a *used to* sentence we often use an auxiliary verb instead of the main verb:

• *I used to have a bicycle but I **don't** anymore / any longer.*
• *I used to like the Beatles and I still **do**!*

When we use the verb *to be* + adjective, we don't repeat the adjective:

• *I used to be fat but I'm not fat anymore.*

7 Reorder the words in these sentences. The first word is underlined.

a doing – still – used – and – <u>I</u> – do – to – sports – hate – I
I used to hate doing sports and I still do .

b to – she – anymore – be – <u>Jo</u> – shy – used – isn't – but
....
....

c Bob – play – they – <u>Tim</u> – and – used – still – soccer – do – to – and
....
....

d used – he – longer – to – for – any – <u>Peter</u> – work – Mrs Warren – but – doesn't
....
....

e make – to – does – laugh – used – and – still – <u>Sam</u> – me – he !
....
....

f anymore – boyfriend – me – he – to – chocolates – <u>My</u> – used – buy – but – doesn't
....
....

Listen and read

Frankenstein

8 a) 📼 What do you know about the story of Frankenstein? Here is an extract from the beginning of the story. A man named Victor Frankenstein has gone to university to study science. At first he writes frequently to his friends and family, then the letters stop. His close friend Henri (the narrator of the story) goes to visit him. Read and / or listen to the text and answer the questions.

LONGMAN CLASSICS

Frankenstein

Mary Shelley

LONGMAN

1 How do you think the narrator (Henri) feels at the end of the extract?

2 How does Frankenstein feel?

3 What was in the bath?

b) Here is a diagram of Frankenstein's apartment. Label the diagram using words from the box.

window bed bath table
living room passage
work table

1 Frankenstein led the way down a long, dark passage to a book-filled room. A bed stood on one side, looking as if nothing had been done to it for days; and on a table near the window were the remains of several meals. There was dust everywhere, and
5 the last of the evening sun shone with difficulty through the dirty windows. There was a rather unpleasant smell.

After I had given him news about his family and told him the reasons for my coming to Ingolstadt, Frankenstein got up and walked about the room excitedly. He didn't seem to be thinking
10 at all about what I had just told him.

"Henri," he said at last. "You have come just at the very moment when I need your help. The great work which I have been doing for the last year is coming to an end, and I shall soon know whether I have been wasting my time or whether I have
15 pushed scientific discovery to new heights." His eyes burned with a strange light. They were like the eyes of a madman.

"My preparations are nearly complete. All I need now are the right conditions for the great experiment to take place. Come," he said, and led the way to a door in a corner of his living room.
20 "You will see what no other man has seen."

He threw open the door, and at once the strange smell which I had noticed before became stronger. It was like the smell of bad meat. I could hardly bear it, but my friend seemed not to notice it, and led the way in.
25 The room was dark, and at first I could only see a mass of wires, glass bottles and jars, and copper and glass pipes. Here and there the blue light of the burners made holes in the darkness. And from those places the sound of boiling liquids could be heard.
30 As my eyes began to see better in the half darkness I saw that this stuff was arranged around a kind of bath in the middle of the room with a wooden work table that went all the way round it. Frankenstein was watching me. There was still this strange excitement in his eyes. "Go on," he said, "look inside. See what
35 I have made."

I bent over the table and looked into the bath. It was filled with a clear liquid. I tried to see deeper into the liquid, but at first all I could see was what looked like hair – fine hair. I bent lower, and as Frankenstein moved a lamp nearer I drew in my
40 breath sharply. It *was* hair – spread out in a golden ring around a face, a head. More. Yes, there was a body in the bath – the body of a man!

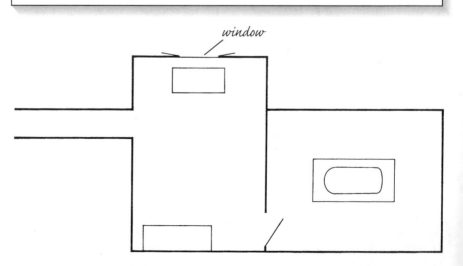

window

Grammar snack

Articles: first and second mention

> **LOOK!**
>
> Notice how *a/an* and *the* are used in the Frankenstein extract:
>
> "Frankenstein led the way ... to (a) book-filled room ... Frankenstein got up and walked about (the) room ..."
>
> • *a* is used the first time we mention something.
> • *the* is used when we mention something for the second (third, fourth, etc.) time.

9 **a)** Read paragraphs five ("He threw open ...") and eight ("I bent over ...") of the Frankenstein extract. Circle seven more examples of this use of *the*. Draw an arrow to show what *the* refers back to.

b) Below is a summary of what happens next in the story. Complete the sentences with *a/an* or *the*.

Frankenstein has made (1) .*a*.... man and he's waiting for (2) .... storm so that he can do (3) .... experiment and bring (4) .... man alive with the help of lightning. Henri helps him with (5) .... experiment and they succeed. However, (6) .... man is (7) .... monster, ugly and horrible, and Frankenstein chases him away.

Shocked and disappointed, Frankenstein gives up his studies and goes back to his family home in Geneva. Henri decides to follow (8) .... monster because he is worried about what it might do next. He discovers that it has gone into a forest and made friends with (9) .... blind man and his children. When Henri visits (10) .... forest several weeks later, he finds (11) .... man's house burned to the ground. Soon after this, he hears that Frankenstein's little brother has been murdered and his nurse is going to be hanged for the crime.

Worried that (12) .... monster is responsible for the child's death, Henri rushes to Geneva, but neither he nor Frankenstein can stop the hanging. They decide to look for (13) .... monster in the mountains and it comes to meet them with (14) .... request. As it tells them (15) .... request, Frankenstein and Henri learn that (16) .... monster was kind at first, but because people were disgusted by its ugly looks, it became more and more cruel. "What I want now is a wife as ugly as I am."

Vocabulary

Scientists and technologists

10 **a)** The people below all work in science and technology. Which subject does each one study? Complete the words.

1 a mathematician   ma *thematics*
2 a scientist   sc _ _ _ _ _
3 a doctor   me _ _ _ _ _ _
4 a psychologist   ps _ _ _ _ _ _ _ _
5 an engineer   en _ _ _ _ _ _ _ _ _
6 an architect   ar _ _ _ _ _ _ _ _ _
7 a geologist   ge _ _ _ _ _

b) The following sentences describe what each person does in their job. Circle the correct verb(s) in each sentence.

1 A scientist *(does)/ makes* experiments and *carries out / makes* research.
2 A psychologist *investigates / looks* people's problems.
3 A doctor *cares / treats* patients and *tells / gives* advice.
4 An architect *draws / writes* plans of buildings.
5 An engineer *carries out / executes* tests on roads and bridges.
6 A mathematician *makes / finds* calculations.
7 A geologist *looks / takes* rock samples and *proves / analyzes* them.

Improve your writing

Spelling of Past Simple forms

11 a) Look again at the rules for spelling the -ing form on page 11 of the Workbook. The rules are the same for spelling the Past Simple form (ending in -ed not -ing). Complete the chart below.

	-ing form	Past Simple
stop	stopping	stopped
train		
plan		
look		
fax		
phone		
offer		
occur		
allow		

> **LOOK!**
>
> Verbs ending in a consonant + y, change y to i and add -ed:
> • cry – cried.
>
> Verbs ending in a vowel + y don't change the y:
> • pray – prayed.
>
> Note: There are two exceptions:
> • say – said, pay – paid.

b) Write the past form of these verbs.

1 try *tried*
2 enjoy
3 hurry
4 play
5 pay
6 employ
7 stay
8 dry
9 apply

Using *when / while / as / during / for* in stories

> **LOOK!**
>
> When we talk about actions or situations that take place at the same time, we can use *when / while / as*:
> • *Maggie hurt her leg **when / while / as** she was jogging.*
> • *I was talking to Penny **when / while / as** you were playing tennis.*
>
> If we are talking about a single event at a particular time, we can only use *when*:
> • *Jane was sixteen **when** she first met David.*
>
> Look at these examples using *during* and *for*:
> • *I'm staying with my cousin **during** the vacation.* (part of the vacation)
> • *I'm staying with my cousin **for** the vacation.* (the whole of the vacation)
>
> Note: we use *during / for* with nouns.

12 a) Below is part of a letter that Jenny wrote to her brother, describing her terrible week. Cross out any words you cannot use.

… And then on Thursday, I took a new client out for lunch at that French restaurant downtown. What a disaster! Everything was fine at first – we got a nice table, but (1) when / while / as / during / for they started playing music, we found we were next to the speakers. We changed tables and ordered our meal. We waited (2) when / while / as / during / for 30 minutes before the waiter brought the wine, and then, (3) when / while / as / during / for he was pouring it, he spilled it all over my client's suit.

She said, "Don't worry," but I could see she was very angry, so (4) when / while / as / during / for we were having the first course, the atmosphere was quite tense. Then (5) when / while / as / during / for we were waiting for the main course, the couple on the next table started having a loud argument!

The worst thing was (6) when / while / as / during / for the check came, I realized I'd left my credit card at home. I felt really embarrassed and in the end she had to pay. And that wasn't all – I said goodbye to her and went to the parking lot and found someone had stolen my car radio (7) when / while / as / during / for the meal.

b) Alan is talking about his weekend. On Saturday he went to his friend Kyra's party. Another friend, Guy, had offered to take him to the party by car.
Complete the sentences with *when / while / as / during / for*.

Well, I was getting dressed (1) *when* Guy called and said he was ill, so I decided to go by train. Unfortunately, (2) .... I was talking on the phone, the cat walked over my clean shirt, so I had to find another one and I was late leaving.

(3) .... I was walking to the station it started snowing and I got very cold. I just missed a train and I had to wait at the station (4) .... half an hour. (5) .... the train finally arrived I was frozen! I was so cold and tired that (6) .... the journey I fell asleep and I missed my station.

Well, I got off at the next stop and decided to walk back to Kyra's. I walked (7) .... half an hour and then I realized I was lost. Luckily I found a phone and telephoned for a taxi. (8) .... I finally arrived at Kyra's house it was nearly midnight and people were going home. What a terrible evening!

module 3

Comparatives and superlatives

1 Sean wants to celebrate his birthday at a nightclub. He has information from three clubs in the city. Complete the sentences in the conversation below with the best form of one of the adjectives from the box.

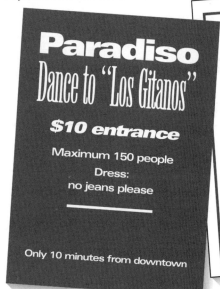

Paradiso
Dance to "Los Gitanos"

$10 entrance

Maximum 150 people

Dress:
no jeans please

Only 10 minutes from downtown

All Nite Long

DJ Max plays your favorite rock & pop

$7 entrance
Maximum 250 people

DOWNTOWN

LIAM'S PLACE

Smokey Joe's Jazz Band

$8.50 entrance
Maximum 75 people

Dress: jacket and tie

Only 15 minutes from the city train station

LIAM'S PLACE

| quiet cheap good central expensive far successful big crowded friendly |

SEAN: I think *All Nite Long* looks good: my friends don't have much money and it's (1) ....*the cheapest*.......... of the three places. It's also

(2) ...., they can take 250 people, and it's

(3) .... so people could get there easily.

MEERA: But *Paradiso* has (4) .... music than *All Nite Long* – they don't have real bands there.

JUSTIN: Actually, I think you should go to *Liam's Place*: I know it's

(5) .... away than the other two, but because it's small, it has a (6) .... atmosphere: the big clubs are too impersonal. Also, it's much (7) .... if people want to talk.

MEERA: Well, *Paradiso* isn't noisy at all. I know it's (8) .... nightclub in town, but for $10 you get live music and a great atmosphere.

JUSTIN: But you know it's much (9) .... than *Liam's Place*: you often can't get a table.

MEERA: Well, that's because it's (10) .... club in the northwest at the moment – everyone wants to go there.

SEAN: Hold on! It's *my* birthday, remember, and I want …

2 You want to rent a place to live. You went to see a house and an apartment and made these notes. Correct the sentences below with a word or phrase from the box (there is one wrong word in each sentence). More than one answer is possible.

House	Apartment
- rent: $600	- rent: $575
- no. of rooms: 8	- no. of rooms: 3
- 45 minutes from station	- 40 minutes from station
- very quiet location: no traffic	- on a busy highway: very noisy!
- not at all clean	- very clean
- furniture: fine	- furniture: terrible!

a bit   a lot   much   slightly   a little

a little / slightly / a bit

a The house is ~~much~~ more expensive than the apartment.

b The apartment is a bit smaller than the house.

c The apartment is much closer to the station than the house.

d The house is a little quieter than the apartment.

e The apartment is slightly cleaner than the house.

f The furniture in the apartment is a bit worse than the furniture in the house.

Comparative and superlative adverbs

LOOK!

Most adverbs that end in *-ly* form the comparative with *more* and the superlative with *most* (Note: **not** *the most*):

- *Could you speak **more clearly** please?*
- *You can find it **most easily** by turning right.*

The following adverbs are the same as the comparative and superlative forms of adjectives.

fast	faster	fastest	hard	harder	hardest
early	earlier	earliest	well	better	best
late	later	latest	badly	worse	worst
long	longer	longest	far	further	furthest
				farther	farthest

3 a) We often use comparative forms of adverbs in requests. Read these sentences and complete the requests.

1 You can't hear what your teacher is saying.
Could you *speak more loudly, please* ....?

2 Your teacher's writing is difficult to read.
Could you ....?

3 You're going to the airport in a taxi and the driver's going very slowly.
Could you ....?

4 Someone's teaching you to use a computer but they explain very quickly.
Could you ....?

5 Your friend usually comes to work or school with you at 8:00 in the morning. Tomorrow you want him to come at 7:30.
Could you ....?

6 Your friend calls, but you are watching your favorite TV program.
Could you ....?

7 You are visiting your grandmother in the hospital. She doesn't want you to leave yet. What does she say?
Could you ....?

b) 📼 Listen to each situation and say the request.

You hear:
You can't hear what your teacher is saying.

You say:
Could you speak more loudly, please?

Comparing things in different ways

4 Look at the following sentences and make one complete sentence, using the word in **bold**.

a   A meal in the Four Seasons restaurant costs $15.
A meal in the Pizza Parlor costs $11.
less
A meal in the Pizza Parlor costs ...*less than a meal*... *in the Four Seasons restaurant* ....

b   The Manor Hotel is $50 a night. The Park Hotel is $75 a night.
expensive
The Manor Hotel isn't ....
....

c   Savewell supermarket has 2,000 customers a day. Pricerite supermarket has 1,500.
more
Savewell supermarket ....
....

d   It takes 40 minutes to cross the city by bus. It takes 25 minutes to cross the city by bike.
less
It takes ....
....

e   There are three trains an hour in the afternoon. There are five trains an hour in the morning.
fewer
There are ....
....

f   The furniture in my sister's apartment is more or less the same as Tim's.
similar
The furniture in my sister's apartment ....
....

g   The Guggenheim Museum in Bilbao is made mostly of metal. The Guggenheim Museum in New York looks like a concrete parking garage.
different
The Guggenheim Museum in New York ....
....

h   Phil's apartment has four rooms and a balcony. My apartment's opposite his, and it has four rooms and a balcony, too.
same
My apartment's ....

Vocabulary

Places around town

5 a) Find eight more words in the word square for places around town (the words go across and down). Use the clues below to help you.

A	N	T	I	Q	U	E	S	H	O	P	B
C	A	O	G	R	N	D	B	K	S	G	C
E	R	S	J	A	U	F	Q	I	T	B	O
S	T	A	D	I	U	M	T	L	A	F	N
H	G	L	M	C	K	D	G	R	T	P	C
T	A	X	I	S	T	A	N	D	I	B	E
J	L	P	B	O	E	O	H	A	O	D	R
F	L	O	R	I	S	T	S	C	N	J	T
N	E	E	D	F	R	I	B	M	E	F	H
D	R	Y	C	L	E	A	N	E	R	S	A
G	Y	C	I	A	H	K	A	E	S	G	L
S	H	O	P	P	I	N	G	M	A	L	L

1   You take your dirty clothes here for cleaning if you don't want them to get wet: *dry cleaners*

2   You can buy pens, paper, and files here:
s _ _ _ _ _ _ _ _ _

3   You could see a soccer game or a pop concert here:
s _ _ _ _ _ _

4   You can buy and send flowers from here: f_ _ _ _ _ _ _

5   A place where taxis wait together: t _ _ _ s _ _ _ _

6   You can spend a morning or an afternoon looking at an exhibition here: a _ _ g _ _ _ _ _ _

7   A place to listen to an orchestra playing classical music: c _ _ _ _ _ _ h _ _ _

8   If you buy a present here, it will definitely be old and might be expensive: a _ _ _ _ _ _ s _ _ _

9   Lots of stores together, in a covered area:
s _ _ _ _ _ _ _ m _ _ _

b) 📼 Listen to the words and mark the main stress: e.g. dry cleaner's.

c) 📼 Listen to the words in phrases and repeat them.

Grammar snack
Prepositions of place: *at, in, on*

LOOK!

When we think about a place as a point, we use *at*:

●

- *There's someone **at** the door.*
- *You have to change trains **at** Connolly Station, Dublin.*

We use *on* to describe the position of something on a surface:

────●────

- *I think your keys are **on** that shelf.*

We also use *on* when we think about a place as a point on a line:

────●────

- *Budapest is **on** the river Danube.*

We use *in* when something is in a three-dimensional space:

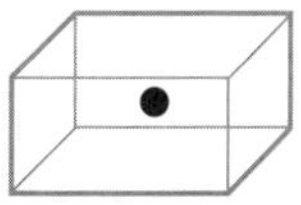

- *He's **in** the bathroom.*

6 Complete the sentences below with *in, on,* or *at*.

Rosaria lives (1) ....*in*.... Salerno, (2) .... Italy. It's a port (3) .... the southwest coast. She lives (4) .... Salerno's downtown (5) .... Via Nizza 244, (6) .... a huge apartment (7) .... the top floor of a modern building. Her family live very close to her: her sister and brother-in-law live (8) .... the end of her street and her mother lives (9) .... the next street. Rosaria works for an advertising company: her office is (10) .... Corso Vittorio Emanuele, the main shopping street. It's not too far away, so she walks there every day and stops (11) .... her way to have breakfast (12) .... a local café.

Pronunciation
/ð/ and /θ/

7 **a)** Listen to the words in the box (or say them aloud) and complete the chart below.

the thin theater another there thank you
these that third both brother through

/ð/	/θ/
the	*thin*

b) Listen to these sentences and repeat them.

1 The theater's over there.
2 Thank you for these.
3 Both of my brothers are thin.
4 There's another room through there.
5 That's the third one I've seen.

Improve your writing
Punctuation: capital letters

LOOK!

We use a capital letter for:
- people's initials, names, marital status, and job title: *Ms. F. Green, Personnel Manager.*
- the names or initials of companies: *International Chemicals, IBM.*
- the names of places: *New Zealand, Park Road.*
- languages, nationalities, and religions: *Tom speaks Chinese, a Greek statue, Sue's a Buddhist.*
- days, months, and public holidays: *Christmas Day is on Wednesday December 25.*
- the most important words in titles of books, magazines, movies, etc.: *Empire of the Sun.*

8 Find and correct any mistakes in the following sentences.

a I'm meeting professor Allinton on Tuesday Afternoon, aren't I?

b Do you know any good japanese restaurants? Our Managing director, Mr. Hashimoto, is coming over next week.

c *Twenty thousand leagues under the sea* was written by jules verne.

d What are you doing at easter?

Grammar snack

The definite article: places

9 **a)** 📼 Read and /or listen to the "jazz chant," paying attention to the rhythm.

> Where shall we go for our summer vacation?
>
> Europe or Asia or closer to home?
>
> We could try the Bahamas or maybe Jamaica
>
> Go around the UK, or Denmark or Spain.
>
> We could sail the Pacific or even Lake Como
>
> Or go down the Yangtze as far as Shanghai.
>
> Or maybe we ought to try something exciting
>
> Like climbing Mount Fuji or crossing the Alps.
>
>
>
> I have a suggestion: what's wrong with New York?
>
> We could see Brooklyn Bridge and sit in Times Square,
>
> Watch a movie on Broadway and walk down Fifth Avenue.
>
> Central Park's great if the weather stays fine.
>
> Then we'll pick up a taxi from Grand Central Station
>
> To JFK Airport and catch our flight home.
>
> That's what I'd like for my summer vacation -
>
> No mountains or beaches but plenty of fun!
>
>

b) Put the places in the box into the correct column in the chart. Find an example (or examples) from the "jazz chant" for each place.

> continents   groups of islands   single islands
> republics or unions of states   countries
> oceans or seas   lakes   rivers
> single mountains   mountain ranges
> cities / towns   roads / streets / avenues
> squares   bridges   parks   stations   airports

with *the*	without *the*
	continents: Europe, Asia

c) Complete the sentences in the vacation advertisement with *the* if it is necessary.

Winter Breaks with Sunspot Vacations

Visit (1) .... *Australia!*

* Spend the first three days in (2) .... Sydney

* See (3) .... Sydney Harbor Bridge

* Go shopping in (4) .... George Street

* Visit (5) .... Blue Mountains, just outside the city.

* Then go north to (6) .... Whitsunday Islands and practice your diving in (7) .... Pacific Ocean.

* Finally, see the crocodiles from the movie *Crocodile Dundee* in (8) .... Kakadu National Park.

> *This is a once-in-a-lifetime offer!*
> *Fourteen days that you'll never forget.*

* **Call 010-600-4000 now.**

Improve your writing

Postcards

When writing postcards, we often leave out a lot of words to save space:

- ~~We're~~ having a great time...
- ~~The~~ food is wonderful ...

10 **a)** Read postcard A from New York and decide where the words in the box should go. What types of words are usually left out?

> The there are my is ~~We're~~
> We're We'll be The is We

Dear Pete and Sarah,

We're
having a great time here in the Big Apple. Weather wonderful – hot and sunny. Spent most of today shopping – fantastic department stores here: credit card's not looking too healthy! Hoping to do some sightseeing tomorrow – Fifth Avenue, Times Square, etc. Nightlife also incredible ... nobody seems to go to bed!

Back in a couple of weeks,
love Sue and Joe
XXXX

Mr. and Mrs. Hall
3 Park Grove
Leicester
England

(A)

b) Read postcard B from Rome and circle the words that can be left out.

(B)

Dear Sam and Julie,

(We) arrived here a couple of days ago – the hotel is small but comfortable, but the food is not great. We're going on a tour of the whole city tomorrow, then we're planning to try some typical pasta dishes for dinner. We hope your family are all well, we'll see you in September.

Love Mark and Tim

Sam and Julie Foster
School Cottage
Broadwood
Gloucester
England

c) Imagine that you are on vacation. Write a postcard to an English-speaking friend

module 4

Present Perfect Simple and Past Simple

1 Read this interview with Zoe, a singer in a pop group, and circle the best verb form.

I = Interviewer   Z = Zoe

I: Well, it's nearly Christmas and your single's number one in the charts. You must be very pleased.

Z: Oh yes, of course: (1) *it was /* (*it's been*) an incredible year for us – we (2) *already had / 've already had* two number one songs this year and (3) *we did / we've done* a tour of the UK.

I: OK, tell us how it all (4) *started / has started*.

Z: We only (5) *formed / have formed* the group in January, and since then we (6) *spent / 've spent* almost every day together. At first we only (7) *played / have played* other people's songs and we (8) *didn't start / haven't started* writing our own songs until we (9) *found / 've found* our manager, Brian.

I: Uh-huh … so when (10) *was / 's been* your first big concert?

Z: Well, that was in May, and around the same time Brian (11) *helped / 's helped* us to get a recording contract with Sony.

I: Yes, and your album's doing very well in the charts. So what's next?

Z: Well, we're working on some new songs and we (12) *agreed / 've agreed* to do a US tour next summer.

I: Great! Well, we all wish you the best of luck and thank you for coming on the program.

2 Six of the sentences below are wrong. Find the mistakes and correct them.

a   ~~Have you seen~~ the news last night? *Did you see*
b   Carrie's a really close friend – we knew each other for ages.
c   I've had this cold all week.
d   Hello, er … sorry, I forgot your name.
e   Jeff's never broken a promise before.
f   Oh, that's a nice watch. How long did you have it?
g   My secretary was late for work every day last month.
h   Look! It has stopped raining!
i   I see your team's in the final. Did they ever win the cup?
j   We didn't play tennis together since the summer.
k   Have you seen John this morning? We have a meeting together at 11:30.
l   I can't find my keys – has anyone seen them?

3 Read this extract from an article called *Famous Moms and Dads* and complete the sentences with the best form of the verb in parentheses.

"It (1) *was* .... (be) my birthday yesterday: I'm 14 years old. Some people say I'm lucky but I don't think so. Imagine, in my life I (2) .... (go) to eight different schools and I (3) .... (never stay) anywhere long enough to make a best friend. We (4) .... (live) in so many different houses that I can't remember some of them. In fact, last year we (5) .... (move) three times. It's true, there are some good things: I (6) .... (meet) some really famous people and we (7) .... (have) some great vacations – I (8) .... (go) to Disneyland at least four times, but never with Mom and Dad. When I (9) .... (be) young, I always (10) .... (have) a nanny, and she (11) .... (take) me on vacation. I'm staying with my aunt and uncle at the moment because my dad's making a movie in France and my mom (12) .... (go) to Los Angeles."

Present Perfect + *just / yet / already*

> **LOOK!**
>
> Notice the position of *just* and *already*:
> • *John's **just** arrived.*
> *Just* = a short time before now.
> • *"Would you like a sandwich?" "I've **already** eaten, thank you."*
> *Already* = before now and means sooner or earlier than we expected.
> • *"Have you seen that movie **yet**, Tim?"*
> • *Jill hasn't been to the British Museum **yet**.*
> *Yet* = before now. We often use *yet* when we **expect** that the person we are talking about **will** do something. It is used in questions and negatives.

4 Reorder the words in these sentences. The first word is underlined.

a   movie – I – started – the – already – has – think
I think the movie has already started .

b   haven't – my – yet – homework – I– done
....

c   just – married – They – got – 've
....

d   Mark – of – come – the – hospital – yet – Has – out ?
....

e   brother – a – just – My – has – car – bought – new
....

f   Christmas – all – already – Jane – sent – cards – has – her
....

5 **a)** Match a sentence from column A with one from column B to make a dialog.

A		B	
1	Have you phoned Brian yet?	a	Yes, we've already met.
2	You look great.	b	I've already done them.
3	Do you want a drink?	c	No, I haven't had any food yet.
4	What did you think of the video I gave you?	d	Thanks, I've just come back from vacation.
5	Do you know Susie?	e	No thanks, I've already had four beers.
6	Have you tried this pizza? It's really good.	f	I haven't had time to watch it yet.
7	Could you finish those letters by lunchtime?	g	He's just gone out.
8	Have you seen John?	h	Yes, but he wasn't in.

1 ..*h*..   2 ....   3 ....   4 ....

5 ....   6 ....   7 ....   8 ....

b) Now cover up column B. Say the first line of the dialog aloud and try and respond with the second line.

for, since, and ago

6 Complete these sentences with the words in parentheses and either *for*, *since*, *ago*, or nothing (–) in some sentences.

a   Joy's had toothache
for three days .
(*three days*)

b   Frankie last went to the dentist
....
(*six months*)

c   My brother and I started going jogging
....
(*a year*)

d   Jane's been feeling sick
....
(*last night*)

e   I took two aspirins
....
(*this morning*)

f   Pete's been on a diet
....
(*two weeks*)

g   I haven't done any exercise
....
(*months*)

h   We played soccer
....
(*all day yesterday*)

i   I've been doing aerobics
....
(*this time last year*)

j   My mother hasn't been feeling well
....
(*her operation*)

Present Perfect Continuous

7 Circle the best verb form in the following sentences.

a   *I've been knowing /* (*I've known*) Susan for about five years.

b   Mom had to take Tim to the dentist because he's *been breaking / broken* his tooth.

c   My husband *'s been having / 's had* his cellphone for a week and it isn't working.

d   I hope Karen calls soon because Rick *'s been waiting / 's waited* by the phone for hours.

e   We've *been going / gone* to the new sports center since June. Why don't you come and try it?

f   Giuseppina's English is getting much better. She *'s been practicing / 's practiced* a lot recently.

g   You look much slimmer. Have you *been dieting / dieted*?

h   John's boss *has been deciding / has decided* to have a vacation next month.

i   Goodbye and thanks for having us. We've *really been enjoying / enjoyed* this evening.

j   TEACHER: OK, *has everyone been finishing / has everyone finished* the exercise? Fine. Let's go on.

Grammar snack

Articles with *school, college*, etc.

LOOK!

A *Matt went **to school** in Kansas.*
B *His father went **to the** school to see the principal.*

In sentence A Matt is a student and goes to school to study, which is the usual reason (no article).

In sentence B the father is visiting the school building, he doesn't study there (we use *a* or *the*).

Here is another example:
• *Nelson Mandela spent many years **in prison**.*
• *His wife couldn't go **to the prison** very often to visit him.*

Places that follow this rule are: school, college, university, church, court, prison.

8 Look at these sentences and cross out *the* or *a* when they are not necessary.

a   1   "Where's Billy?" "He's still at ~~the~~ school: his lessons don't finish until 4:00."

   2   There's a school very near here.

b   1   I waited in the church for the rain to stop.

   2   "Do you go to the church?" "Yes, every Sunday."

c   1   Jan's going to the court today because she hasn't paid her taxes for five years.

   2   Tourists are allowed to visit the court on Thursday mornings.

d   1   I left the university when I was 21.

   2   My parents came to the university for my graduation day.

e   1   My three years at a college were fantastic.

   2   I went to the college to see an exhibition.

Vocabulary

Describing people's appearance

9 **a)** Complete the chart below with a word or phrase from the box and *He has*, *He wears*, or *He's / His hair's*.

| nice   a rather pointed nose   quite slim   of medium build   going gray |
| quite wavy   not very tall   friendly   casual   a bit overweight   round |
| sparkly eyes   highlighted   good dress sense   colorful   going bald |

Face	Clothes	Build	Hair
He has . . . a rather pointed nose	He . . . wears nice clothes	He's . . .	He's / His hair's . . .

b) Complete these descriptions with words and phrases from the boxes.

1   My uncle Bill's ....*quite tall*............... . He has gray, curly hair and

a ...., ... face. He often wears very

.... and he always looks quite ....

| friendly   round   colorful clothes   nice   ~~quite tall~~ |

2   My grandmother's ....
and she's a little ....
She has a .... face
and white .... hair.
She's getting a bit old now, but she
always wears ....
and she has the most beautiful hands
I've ever seen.

| nice clothes   wavy   overweight |
| not very tall   friendly |

3   My cousin Jim's 18. He's

.... and not

.... He has

long, ... hair

and quite a ....

face. He likes wearing

.... clothes:

jeans and T-shirts, usually.

| of medium build   very tall |
| pointed   wavy   casual |

c) In your notebook write a description **either** of someone famous **or** of someone in your class. Show it to your teacher.

Pronunciation

/ɪ/, /iː/, and /aɪ/

> **LOOK!**
>
> Compare these three sounds:
>
> /ɪ/: a b<u>i</u>t to f<u>i</u>n<u>i</u>sh
>   /ɪ/   /ɪ/ /ɪ/
>
> /iː/: to r<u>ea</u>d p<u>eo</u>ple
>   /iː/   /iː/
>
> /aɪ/: m<u>y</u> wh<u>i</u>te
>   /aɪ/   /aɪ/

10 **a)** 🔲 Listen to the phrases below (or say them aloud) and write the correct symbol in the spaces.

1 his hair's q<u>ui</u>te th<u>i</u>ck
      /aɪ/   /ɪ/

2 he's of m<u>e</u>dium b<u>ui</u>ld
       / /   / /

3 she has gr<u>ee</u>n <u>eye</u>s
       / /   / /

4 her hair's h<u>i</u>ghl<u>i</u>ghted
       / / / /

5 she's pr<u>e</u>tty and very sl<u>i</u>m
       / /   / /

6 she has a sw<u>ee</u>t sm<u>i</u>le
       / /   / /

7 he's k<u>i</u>nd and rather sh<u>y</u>
       / /   / /

8 he's much th<u>i</u>nner now he's in
   his t<u>ee</u>ns   / /
       / /

b) Listen to the phrases again and repeat them.

Listen and read

Tom Cruise

11 🔲 Read and / or listen to this biography of the movie star Tom Cruise and mark the statements below *T* (true) or *F* (false).

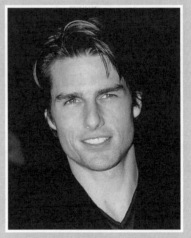

Born in Syracuse, New York, on July 3, 1962, Tom Cruise had a difficult childhood. His parents divorced when he was twelve, and in the first eleven years of his life his family moved a total of seven times. He had problems at school, partly because he never stayed in one place long enough to make friends and partly because he suffered from dyslexia and found reading very hard. As a teenager he couldn't decide whether to become a priest or a wrestler, but at the age of eighteen he chose acting as a career.

His first movie *Endless Love*, in 1981, was followed quickly in the same year by *Taps* in which he had a strong supporting role as an angry young cadet. Over the next few years he made a name for himself in a series of fairly successful movies, often playing attractive "boy-next-door" types. His big break came in 1986 in the hit *Top Gun*, where he played a rebellious fighter pilot with a killer smile.

By the late 1980s magazines were calling him "easily the most powerful star of his generation" because of his more serious roles in *Rain Man*, in 1988, opposite Dustin Hoffman, and *Born on the Fourth of July*, which was made in the following year. For this movie he received his first Oscar nomination for Best Actor for his powerful performance as the antiwar hero Ron Kovic. People who have worked with him say he's a perfectionist, preparing carefully for each role, and focusing 100 percent while in the studio. Success continued in the 1990s with movies such as *Mission Impossible* and *Eyes Wide Shut*. He is now one of the few actors who receives more than 20 million dollars a picture.

Cruise is a very private man, who rarely gives interviews. His personal life has had its ups and downs. In 1987 he married actress Mimi Rogers who was several years older than him, but the marriage ended in divorce in 1990. In the same year he married his costar from *Days of Thunder*, red-headed actress Nicole Kidman. Both of them are members of the Church of Scientology, but Cruise has always refused to answer questions about his religion.

Whatever happens in his private life, people will remember him as one of the most charismatic actors in modern movie history and many will probably agree with *People* magazine in 1997 when they chose him as one of the fifty most beautiful people in the world.

a Tom Cruise was very successful at school. ..*F*..

b He always wanted to become an actor. .....

c He played the star part in *Taps*. .....

d *Top Gun* was his most successful early movie. .....

e He was nominated for an Oscar for *Born on the Fourth of July*. .....

f He is a very hard worker. .....

g He hardly ever gives interviews. .....

h He got married to Nicole Kidman in 1991. .....

Improve your writing

Punctuation: commas

> **LOOK!**
>
> We put a comma (,) in a sentence to show a short pause.
>
> In a list, we use a comma instead of *and* or *or*:
> • *He lived in France, Italy, Belgium, and Spain.*
>
> When we join two short sentences with a conjunction, e.g. *and*, *but*, or *so,* we often use a comma before the conjunction:
> • *He moved to France, but he never forgot his friends in England.*
>
> If the sentence is short, a comma is not always necessary:
> • *He loved Paris but I didn't.*
>
> Notice where we put the commas in direct speech:
> • *"I'll buy the tickets," he said.*
> • *She said, "It's OK, I have lots of money."*

12 **a)** Insert commas where necessary in these sentences.

1 I'm not very keen on jazz⊙ blues⊙ or rock music.

2 Steve practices his guitar every day and has guitar lessons twice a week.

3 I don't know much about the Beatles but I like their music a lot.

4 I like going to rock concerts but the tickets can be really expensive so I don't go often.

5 "I thought they were rubbish" Naomi said as we came out of the concert.

6 There were four members of the group: John Paul George and Ringo.

7 Jorge said "You can borrow my guitar."

8 "Come on" Paddy said "or we'll be late."

9 "I can get tickets for January 12 13 or 15."

10 The music was very loud but quite good.

b) In the following extract Bob Geldof, a famous rock star, talks about his meeting with Mother Teresa of Calcutta. Read the text and insert commas where necessary.

We sat in the airport till Mother Teresa came in. I felt hot⊙ tired⊙ and a bit nervous. I wanted to kiss her when I met her but she didn't let me. She told me about her work in Ethiopia. She and her sisters took care of sick people and homeless children. I wanted to help them and I told her about my music.

Then I said "I'll give a concert in India for you."

"No. God will give us what we need." She turned to one of the important people nearby.

"I saw two big old palaces in the city" she said. "Will you give me them for my homeless children?"

"I'm not sure about palaces but we can find you a house."

"Two houses" said Mother Teresa.

"Two houses."

I understood that Mother Teresa could ask for anything and she would get it. She was all goodness. She wanted nothing for herself. Then she took my hand and said "I can do something you can't do and you can do something I can't do but we both have to do it."

module 5

will and *won't*

1 Complete these sentences with *will* or *won't* and a verb from the box.

> take   get   like   ~~be ready~~   come   be   need
> agree   pass   send

a   I need these shoes on Saturday.
    Will they be ready (they) by then?

b   You can invite your ex-girlfriend to the party, but
    I'm sure she ....

c   We .... to order the flowers at
    least two weeks before the wedding.

d   .... (you) late tonight?

e   I don't think you should buy Mom those gloves, she
    .... them.

f   So, the exam's in June. When ....
    (they) us the results?

g   Don't forget to take a sweater: I expect it
    .... cold later.

h   Stop worrying about the exam – you
    .... easily.

i   Why do you want to leave so early? It
    .... very long to get there.

j   You can ask her to type your work but I don't think
    she ....

going to

2 Complete these conversations with the correct form of *going to* and a suitable verb where necessary (short answers may be possible).

a   A: It's my 18th birthday in June.
    B: *Are you going to have* a party?
    A: I haven't decided yet.

b   A: My brother's just heard that he's lost his job.
    B: Oh no! What .... ?
    A: I think he's planning to travel for a while.

c   A: Are you really going
       to give up smoking?
    B: Yes, ...
       I threw my last pack
       of cigarettes away
       yesterday.

d   A: Do you have any plans for the weekend?
    B: Well, David and I ....
       a movie on Sunday night.
    A: Oh, which one?

e   A: Are you nervous about
       making a speech at the
       wedding?
    B: Yes, but ....
       ....
       about it anymore.
    A: No – thinking about it
       will make you more
       nervous.

f   A: Lisa's really in love with Alain, isn't she?
       .... him?
    B: I hope so. He'd be the perfect husband for her.

g   A: I heard that the council has bought that land
       behind the movie theater to build on.
    B: Oh really? What ....
       there?
    A: A new shopping mall, I think.

h   A: Are you and Annie going to have a vacation this
       year?
    B: No, ... We have
       no money.

Present Continuous for future arrangements

3 **a)** Who do the datebooks below belong to? Choose from the box.

> a university student   a politician   a business person
> a dentist   a pop singer

A ....   B ....

TUESDAY 8TH

9:00	*Mrs. Philips, Ben & Sally – checkup*
10:00	*Mr. Lord – extraction*
11:00	
12:00	*Susan Kennedy*
1:00	
2:00	
3:00	*afternoon off*
4:00	
5:00	

TUESDAY 8TH

10:30	Shakespeare lecture
12:00	Daniella – lunch
1:00	squash with Paul
3:00	meeting with Professor Livesy to discuss essay

b) Use the prompts to make complete sentences with the correct form of the Present Continuous.

Datebook A

A: Hello, Mr. Haines's surgery.
B: Yes, hello ... could the dentist see my daughter? She has terrible toothache.
A: Well, he / see / patients all morning.
   (1) *Well, he's seeing patients all morning* ....
B: Um ... what about the afternoon?
A: I'm sorry, he / have / the afternoon off, but he could see you at one o'clock.
   (2) ....
B: Oh, thank you, I'll bring her then.

Datebook B

C: I need to talk to you. Can we meet sometime today?
D: Well, I'm quite busy: I / go / to a lecture this morning and I / meet / Daniella for lunch.
   (3) ....
   ....
C: What / you / do in the afternoon?
   (4) .... ?
D: Well, I / play / squash until 3:00, then I have a meeting.
   (5) ....
   you / do / anything in the evening? I'm free then.
   (6) ....
C: No, that's fine.

Other ways of talking about the future

4 Use the prompts to make complete sentences in these dialogs.

a My nephew Justin's leaving school in July.
   Oh, what / he / intending / do / after that?
   Oh, what is he intending to do ......
   after that .... ?

b What time are your grandparents coming?
   They / due / arrive / at about six.
   ....
   ....

c I'm going to spend the summer in Turkey.
   Really? Where / you / planning / stay?
   ....
   .... ?

d I hear you've bought a new house.
   Yes, we / hoping / move / next month.
   ....
   ....

e Jeannie looks a bit worried.
   I know, she / about / take / her driver's test.
   ....
   ....

f What are you going to do with the money you won in the lottery?
   Well, I / thinking / buy / a new car with some of it.
   ....
   ....

g Matt's been practicing the piano a lot, hasn't he?
   Yes, he / determined / win / the competition.
   ....
   ....

Future clauses with *if*, *when*, etc.

5 Match a question from column A with an answer from column B to make a dialog.

A		B
a	Will you call me tonight?	1 He'll try to come if he's free.
b	Could you let Sandra have the plane tickets next week?	2 Not yet. I'll finish them once I find my pen.
c	Have you finished writing those invitations?	3 I don't know yet, I'll know more after I phone the hospital.
d	Can you ask Tim to photocopy these letters?	4 Yes, I'll phone you as soon as I get home.
e	Is Jack coming to the party?	5 Yes – I won't need it until the weekend.
f	What time do you expect to be home?	6 Of course, I'll mail them to her when I get them.
g	Do you have the new *Oasis* CD?	7 I'll be on the six o'clock train unless the meeting finishes late.
h	Could I borrow your tennis racket?	8 Yes, I'll make sure he does it before he goes home.
i	Was your friend hurt in the accident?	9 Yes, it's great. I'll play it for you next time you come to my house.

a ..*4*.. b .... c .... d .... e ....

f .... g .... h .... i ....

6 Look at these sentences and make one complete sentence, using the word in **bold**.

a We're going to play again. I'll beat you then.
next time

I'll beat *you next time we play* .

b You'll be in Madrid again. Phone me then.
when

Phone me ....

....

c It's going to get dark soon. Let's stop now.
before

Let's stop ....

....

d I'm moving next week. Then I'll give you my phone number.
after

I'll give ....

....

e That movie will come out soon. I'd like to see it then.
as soon as

I'd like ....

....

f Maurizio'll finish university soon. He hopes to get a job then.
once

Maurizio hopes ....

....

g The taxi'll come in a few minutes. I'll wait with you.
until

I'll wait ....

....

Grammar snack

Prepositions of time for the future

> **LOOK!**
>
> We use *on* with days and dates:
> * *I'm seeing him on* | *Tuesday afternoon.*
> | *February 6.*
>
> We use *in* for a period longer or shorter than a day.
> * *We'll finish it in November / the afternoon / 2001.*
>
> We use *in* for a period between now and a future time:
> * *We're meeting in two days.*
>
> We use *at* for points in the future and public holidays:
> * *We'll stop at midnight.*
> * *I'm going to see my parents at Easter.*
>
> There is no preposition with *next*, *this*, or *the*:
> * *This time next week I'll be on vacation.*
> * *I'll finish my course the year after next.*

7 **a)** Look at the expressions in the box and put them into the correct column in the chart below.

> a few minutes   the year after next   2010   Saturday night   Sunday
> this time next year   midday   December 1   two weeks   Christmas
> next month   a moment   lunchtime   7:30   three weeks
> this time tomorrow   my birthday   next Saturday   a month
> Wednesday evening   the day after tomorrow

in	on	at	–
a few minutes			

b) Complete these sentences so that they are true for you (talking about the future).

1 This time tomorrow ....

2 On Saturday night ....

3 On my birthday ....

4 At eight o'clock tomorrow morning ....

5 ﹑In a few minutes ....

6 The day after tomorrow ....

Pronunciation

/ɜː/, /ɒː/, and /oʊ/

> **LOOK!**
>
> Compare these sounds:
>
> | <u>cur</u>l | c<u>a</u>ll |
> |---|---|
> | /ɜː/ | /ɒː/ |
> | b<u>ou</u>ght | b<u>oa</u>t |
> | /ɒː/ | /oʊ/ |
> | <u>gir</u>l | g<u>oa</u>l |
> | /ɜː/ | /oʊ/ |

8 **a)** 🔳 Listen to the pairs of words in the chart and repeat them.

/ɜː/	/ɒː/	/oʊ/
surfed	soft	
weren't		won't
hurt	hall	
curl	call	
learn		loan
work	walk	
	law	low
	caught	coat
burn		bone

b) 🔳 Now listen and write the word you hear.

1 *loan* ....

2 ....

3 ....

4 ....

5 ....

6 ....

7 ....

8 ....

9 ....

10 ....

Vocabulary

Jobs

9 **a)** The pictures below show different jobs. Rearrange the mixed-up letters to make the name of each job.

1 ocnacntuat   a.*ccountant*.................

2 realwy   l...............................

3 nirdeegs   d.............................

4 rarteyces   s............................

5 enegrine   e.............................

6 pitersnotice   r..........................

7 retrucle   l..............................

8 hicretcat   a.............................

LOOK!

You can use your English–English dictionary to help you with word stress. The dictionary shows stress with the mark ' in front of the stressed syllable:

> **teach·er** /'tiːtʃər/ n [C] someone whose job is to teach: *Miss Tindale's my favorite teacher*
>
> **re·port·er** /rɪ'pɔːrtər/ n [C] someone who writes about events for a newspaper, radio, or television
>
> **pol·i·ti·cian** /pɑlɪ'tɪʃən/ n [C] someone who works in politics, especially an elected member of a parliament or similar institution

It's a good idea to mark the stress when you learn a new word. You can do this with a circle over the stressed syllable:

● teacher   ● politician   ● reporter

---

b) Using these extracts from the *Longman Dictionary of Contemporary English*, mark the stress ● on the jobs in a).

> **ac·coun·tant** /ə'kaʊntənt/ n [C] someone whose job is to keep and check financial accounts
>
> **law·yer** /'lɔːjər/ n [C] someone whose job is to advise people about laws, write formal agreements, or represent people in court
>
> **de·sign·er¹** /dɪ'zaɪnər/ n [C] someone whose job is to make plans or patterns for clothes, furniture, equipment, etc.: *a dress designer*
>
> **ar·chi·tect** /'ɑːrkɪtekt/ n [C] someone whose job is to design buildings
>
> **se·re·ta·ry** /'sekrəteri/ n [C] someone who works in an office typing letters, keeping records, arranging meetings, etc.
>
> **en·gi·neer¹** /endʒɪ'nɪr/ n [C] someone who designs the way roads, bridges, machines, etc. are built
>
> **re·cep·tion·ist** /rɪ'sepʃənɪst/ n [C] someone whose job is to welcome and deal with people arriving in a hotel or office building, visiting a doctor, etc.
>
> **lecturer** /'lektʃərər/ n [C] someone who gives a lecture: *a brilliant lecturer*

c) 🔊 Listen and repeat the words, paying attention to the stress.

Adjectives to describe jobs

10 **a)** Match an adjective from column A with a definition from column B.

	A		B
1	tiring	a	making you feel very sad
2	stressful	b	making you feel happy and satisfied because you feel you are doing something useful or important
3	challenging	c	making you feel that you want to sleep or rest
4	varied	d	producing or using new or imaginative ideas, results, etc.
5	creative	e	involving different kinds of things or people
6	depressing	f	makes you worry a lot
7	rewarding	g	difficult in an interesting or enjoyable way

1 ..*c*...   2 ....   3 ....   4 ....

5 ....   6 ....   7 ....

b) The adjectives are written in phonemic script below. Notice where the stressed syllable is. Complete each line with the correct adjective, marking the stress ●.

1 *depressing* ●
/dɪˈpresɪŋ/

2 ....
/ˈstresfʊl/

3 ....
/krɪˈjeɪtɪv/

4 ....
/ˈtʃæləndʒɪŋ/

5 ....
/ˈtaɪrɪŋ/

6 ....
/rɪˈwɔːdɪŋ/

7 ....
/ˈverɪd/

Real life

Formal telephone conversations

11 a) You are phoning Mrs Leeson, at Henderson Insurance. If you can't speak to her personally, you need her to phone you back. Complete the dialog with suitable questions and responses.

A: Good afternoon, Henderson Insurance, Pam speaking. How can I help?

B: Good afternoon, could *I speak to Mrs. Leeson, please* ....?

A: Just a moment, I'll connect you.

C: Hello, Mrs. Leeson's office, Sandy speaking.

B: Hello, could .... ?

C: I'll just see if she's available. Can I ask who's calling?

B: ....

C: One moment, please (*pause*). Hello, I'm afraid she's not in the office at the moment. Would you like her to call you back?

B: ....

C: Can I take your number?

B: ....

C: Right, I'll get her to call you back as soon as she comes in.

B: ....

C: Goodbye.

b) You are phoning International School to find out information about their English courses for executives. Leave a message on the answering machine.

Answering machine message: This is the International School answering service. We're sorry there's no one available to take your call. Please leave your message after the tone. If you would like information about courses, please leave your name and address and we'll send you our brochure. Thank you. (*tone*)

....

....

....

c) 📼 Listen to some possible answers for a) and b).

d) 📼 Now try to respond in the spaces on the cassette, without looking at your book.

You hear:
Good afternoon, Henderson Insurance, Pam speaking. How can I help?

You say:
Good afternoon, could I speak to Mrs. Leeson, please?

Improve your writing

Apostrophes

> **LOOK!**
>
> We use apostrophes:
> - to show a missing letter or letters: *I am – I'm, He has – He's.*
> - to show possession with nouns: *Robin's pen.*
>
> Notice:
> - *the girl's mother* = one girl.
>   *the girls' mother* = more than one girl.
> - With irregular plurals, the apostrophe goes before the -s: *the children's game.*
> - We don't use apostrophes with possessive pronouns and adjectives: *hers, its, ours, theirs.*

12 Insert an apostrophe where necessary in these sentences.

a I read your pen pals letter – she sounds really nice.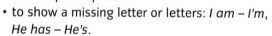

b This is the boys bedroom. Theyre both at school at the moment.

c Its a nice day, isnt it?

d Whose is this? I think its hers.

e Whos that at the reception desk?

f The companys lost all its best designers.

g Hes leaving in a year.

h I have five years experience in advertising.

module 6

-ed / -ing adjectives

1 a) Complete these sentences with an adjective from the box.

depressed / depressing   frightened / frightening
embarrassed / embarrassing   excited / exciting
disappointed / disappointing   annoyed / annoying
surprised / surprising

1   Rob's starting his new job tomorrow, isn't he?

Yes, I think he's quite *excited* but very nervous too.

2   We were very .... to hear that Ann and Tom are going to get married. We didn't think that she liked him.

3   What did you think of the movie?

Actually, I thought it was quite .... I expected it to be better.

4   I was really .... because I couldn't remember his name and it was the third time I'd met him.

5   Some parents thought the movie *Jurassic Park* was too .... for children under five years old.

6   Sally gets very .... when people are late for meetings.

7   Mrs. Dudley's really .... Her cat died last week.

b) Complete the following sentences so that they are true for you.

1   I find .... terrifying.

2   I get very annoyed when ....

....

3   I'm always pleased when ....

....

4   When I get excited I usually ....

5   I find .... really boring.

6   I don't find .... shocking.

7   When I feel depressed I usually ....

Grammar snack

Prepositions after *-ed / -ing* adjectives

Adjectives can be followed by prepositions.
A good dictionary shows you these: *depressed about*

> **de·pressed** /dɪˈprest/ *adj* a) feeling very unhappy: *She felt lonely and depressed.*| **[+ about]** *Carter seemed depressed about the situation*

2 a) Use these extracts from the *Longman Dictionary of Contemporary English* to find the prepositions that follow the adjectives below.

> **bored** /bɔːrd/ *adj* tired and impatient because you do not think something is interesting, or because you have nothing to do: *Children easily get bored.*| **[+ with]** *I'm bored with the same old routine day after day*
>
> **con·fused** /kənˈfjuːzd/ *adj* unable to understand clearly what someone is saying or what is happening: *I am totally confused. Could you explain that again?*| **[+ about]** *If you are confused about anything, phone my office*
>
> **dis·ap·point·ed** /dɪsəˈpɔɪntɪd/ *adj* sad because something you hoped for did not happen, or because someone or something was not as good as expected: *Dad seemed more disappointed than angry.*| **[+ about]** *Nathan's really disappointed about not being able to go*
>
> **fright·ened** /ˈfraɪtnd/ *adj* feeling afraid: *a frightened animal*| **[+ of]** *I was frightened of being left by myself in the house*
>
> **in·terest·ed** /ˈɪntrəstɪd/ *adj* giving a lot of attention to something because you want to find out more about it: **[+ in]** *I'm not really interested in politics*
>
> **sur·prised** /sərˈpraɪzd/ *adj* having a feeling of surprise: *Mr. Benson looked surprised when I told him I was leaving*| **[+ at/by]** *We were all surprised at Sue's outburst*
>
> **wor·ried** /ˈwʌrid/ *adj* unhappy because you keep thinking about a problem or are anxious about something: *Don't look so worried – we'll find him.*| **[about]** *She's so worried about her exams*
>
> **em·bar·rassed** /ɪmˈbærəst/ *adj* ashamed, nervous, or uncomfortable in a social situation: *I managed to spill water on one of the guests – I was so embarrassed!*| **[+ about]** *At about the age of twelve, girls start feeling embarrassed about changing their clothes in front of other people*

1   bored *with*

2   confused ....

3   disappointed ....

4   frightened ....

5   interested ....

6   surprised ....

7   worried ....

8   embarrassed ....

b) Rewrite these sentences using the correct preposition.

1 The economy is depressing.
I'm *depressed about the economy* .

2 Stella found his behavior surprising.
Stella was ....

3 Adrian's job interview is worrying him.
Adrian's ....

4 Missing the party was really disappointing.
I was ....

5 Your suggestions for the project are very interesting.
We're very ....

6 Henry's job is really boring.
Henry is ....

7 Roy found his big nose embarrassing.
Roy was ....

8 My daughter finds the dark frightening.
My daughter's ....

9 The reason for the meeting is confusing.
I'm ....

The passive

3 Look at the following sentences and write questions using the passive form.

a George was taken to the hospital because he had a heart attack. (ask *why*)
Why was George taken to the hospital ?

b The prisoner was shot at seven o'clock this morning. (ask *when*)
....?

c Tickets for the concert are sold at all large music stores. (ask *where*)
....?

d The new theater will be built in five years. (ask *when*)
....?

e The article was written by Urma Mackintyre. (ask *who by*)
....?

f The plant has been moved because it wasn't getting enough light. (ask *why*)
....?

g Portuguese is spoken in Brazil. (ask *where*)
....?

h Napoleon was known as Boney. (ask *what*)
....?

i The movie was directed by Zeffirelli. (ask *who by*)
....?

j Forty-seven people have been injured. (ask *how many*)
....?

4 Complete these sentences with the correct passive form of the verb in parentheses.

a In the UK psychology .... *is taught* .... in universities but not usually in schools. (*teach*)

b The body of a young man .... in the river yesterday. (*find*)

c Thirty-five cars .... from downtown since January. (*steal*)

d Where .... the next Olympics .... ? (*hold*)

e Alcoholic drinks .... to children under 16. (*not sell*)

f .... the bridge .... a long time ago? (*build*)

g I'm sorry, but dinner .... in the price of an overnight stay. (*not include*)

h .... the vegetables .... immediately after you pick them? (*freeze*)

i The hole in my roof .... next Friday. (*repair*)

j Mary .... about the accident yet. (*not tell*)

5 Read these texts and complete the sentences with the best form (active or passive) of the verbs in **bold** below each text.

A

"... and this is the last stage of the production process. As you know, Swift sneakers are very expensive, and the reason they (1) _cost_ .... so much is that they (2) .... of the highest quality leather. We (3) .... over 10 million sneakers to countries all around the world and our shoes (4) .... by all types of people, from top athletes to children at school."

| wear make cost export |

B

"... and that (1) .... a track from the latest CD by Didi Brown. The songs (2) .... by Didi herself when she (3) .... in Ireland last year. The CD goes on sale next week and half the money from the sales (4) .... to the 'Children in Need' fund."

| write give stay be |

C

"This is the new Primera Consul, sir. As you can see it (1) .... The engine is much more powerful now and it (2) .... much quieter. There's a sunroof that (3) .... when you press this button, and all models now (4) .... with a stereo radio/CD player included."

| make come redesign open |

Vocabulary
Movies, TV, and newspapers

6 a) Look at the clues below and find the words in the word square.

D	O	C	U	M	E	N	T	A	R	Y	Z
A	S	H	P	W	N	E	H	X	Y	I	L
N	W	A	R	Q	C	A	R	T	O	O	N
C	B	R	U	M	U	E	I	O	E	H	X
K	I	S	H	E	A	D	L	I	N	E	S
P	E	P	R	T	Y	N	L	A	Q	T	C
H	S	O	A	P	O	P	E	R	A	A	I
M	I	N	E	R	D	Q	R	M	R	L	E
M	U	S	I	C	A	L	P	L	T	K	N
V	A	L	W	I	N	G	R	X	I	S	C
G	I	L	S	A	H	A	I	T	C	H	E
A	D	X	Y	A	B	M	P	E	L	O	S
S	E	W	E	L	R	E	V	I	E	W	O

1 A serious TV program about real topics.
  A d _ocumentary_

2 A movie about countries fighting.   A w _ _ movie

3 A movie where the characters are not real. They are drawn.   A c _ _ _ _ _ _

4 A piece of writing in a newspaper or a magazine.
  An a _ _ _ _ _ _

5 A TV program that is on two or three times a week with a continuing story about people's lives.
  A s _ _ _ o _ _ _ _

6 A play or movie with lots of singing and dancing.
  A m _ _ _ _ _ _

7 Titles of newspaper stories that are printed in large letters at the top of the stories.   h _ _ _ _ _ _ _ _

8 A short word for *advertisement*. An a _

9 A TV program where famous people are interviewed about their lives and interests.   A t _ _ _ s _ _ _

10 A very exciting movie about dangerous, frightening, or mysterious events.   A t _ _ _ _ _ _ _

11 You can win prizes in this type of TV program.
  A g _ _ _ show.

12 A movie about events that take place in the future or in space.   A s _ _ _ _ _ _ -fiction movie.

13 An article giving an opinion about a new movie, play, book, or exhibition.   A r _ _ _ _ _

b) 🖭 Listen to the words and repeat them.

Grammar snack

Prepositions for talking about books, movies, etc.

LOOK!

We use these prepositions for talking about books:

- *in* a book
- *on* page 10
- *in* the first chapter
- *at* the beginning / end
- *on* the front / back cover

When we want to talk about where something takes place we say:

- *Where's it on?* | It's
  | The movie's | *on at the* + place
  | The concert's

It's *on at the* Star Theater.

7 a) Complete the phrases in the chart below with the correct preposition.

Newspapers	Movies	TV / Radio
in a newspaper	...... a movie	...... TV / the radio
...... the sports section	...... the first / last scene	...... CNN / Radio Brussels
...... page 2	...... the beginning / end	...... a program
...... the front / back page		...... the news
...... an advertisement		

b) Use the prompts to make complete answers to these questions.

1 Is there a photograph of the writer?   Yes / it / be / back cover.
   Yes, it's on the back cover ....

2 What happened to the hero in the play?   He / kill / last scene.
   ....

3 Where are the answers to these exercises?   They / be / page 65.
   ....

4 What's on TV tonight?   There / be / good movie / Channel 4 at 8:30.
   ....

5 Where is the Picasso Exhibition on?   It / be / the National Gallery.
   ....

6 Where did you hear about the train accident?   radio / last night.
   ....

7 I can't find the TV guide in this newspaper.   It / be / back page.
   ....

8 Where are the movie reviews?   I think they / be / entertainment movie section.
   ....

9 Was John on TV last night?   Yes, didn't you see him? He / be / *Break or Bust*.
   ....

Pronunciation

/f/, /v/, and /w/

LOOK!

Compare these three sounds:

/f/: <u>f</u>ast, <u>ph</u>rase
/v/: <u>v</u>ery, lea<u>v</u>e
/w/: <u>wh</u>ere, flo<u>w</u>er

8 a) 📼 Listen to these sentences and mark the /f/, /v/, and /w/ sounds.

1 I was <u>f</u>ascinated by the
       /f/
   inter<u>v</u>ie<u>w</u> on T<u>V</u> last night.
       /v//w/   /v/

2 Ken goes swimming every week.

3 Phone me if you're confused about anything.

4 I'm terrified of storms, especially when I'm outside.

5 The weather forecast says it's going to get worse.

6 Philip drove over 1,000 miles last week.

7 Don't forget to switch off the photocopier before you leave the office.

8 Do you believe in love at first sight?

9 That movie got one of the worst reviews I've ever read.

10 I've just finished my homework. Can I go out?

b) Listen again and repeat the sentences.

Listen and read

Letters to a TV magazine

9 **a)** 🖭 Read and / or listen to these letters. Which of the letters are positive and which are negative?

Ⓐ

Well done ABC for the brilliant series <u>City Mysteries</u>. The characters were really convincing and the stories completely believable. I was so disappointed when it finished. When will the next series be made? Are there any plans to release it on video?

G. Brown

Newtown

Ⓒ

Dear Editor,

I was really upset when I heard that the cartoon hour won't be shown on Saturday mornings any more. My brother and I used to watch it every week, especially *Superteenagers*, and we definitely don't like the boring gardening program you've put on instead. Please, please, please give us back our cartoons!

David (aged 12)

Stonebridge

Ⓓ

This was the scene in my living room last Saturday: my two daughters were excited about staying up late that night to see <u>Popswap</u> their favorite program, and I was looking forward to a calm half hour. Imagine how disappointed we all were when we heard that our program had been replaced by <u>Soccer Crazy</u>. I understand that there was a very important game that night, but I do not understand why it needed a half-hour introductory discussion!

Julie Grey

Cardiff

Ⓑ

I would like to congratulate Channel 6 for its marvelous documentary about the life and work of Louis Armstrong. His wonderful voice was loved by millions of people and he was a truly international entertainer. His death was a loss to all of us but his songs will live forever.

S. Gascoigne

Queensborough

1 Letter A: *positive*............
2 Letter B: ....
3 Letter C: ....
4 Letter D: ....

b) Mark these statements *T* (true) or *F* (false).

1 The series *City Mysteries* wasn't as good as G. Brown expected it to be. ...*F*.

2 G. Brown would like to have a copy of *City Mysteries*. .....

3 Louis Armstrong entertained people all over the world. .....

4 S. Gascoigne thought the acting in the Louis Armstrong program was really good. .....

5 There's a new gardening program on TV on Saturday mornings. .....

6 *Superteenagers* are real people. .....

7 *Popswap* was on at an earlier time than usual. .....

8 Julie Grey was interested in the soccer discussion. .....

Improve your writing

Linking ideas without repeating yourself

> **LOOK!**
>
> To avoid repeating words and expressions that have been used before, we often use:
>
> • possessive adjectives (*his, its, their*, etc.)
> • pronouns (*it, she, we*, etc.)
> • different vocabulary, e.g.
>
> Simon Strange's new novel is a murder mystery. The book is his sixth and it will go on sale next week.

10 **a)** What do the circled words refer back to in this letter? Draw arrows (←◯).

6 Beech Avenue
Doncaster DO3 9BS

April 15, 2004

Dear Sir/Madam,

I was really pleased to see that you're repeating the Girlz 'n' Boyz show on MTV. It's the best music program around and has probably the most interesting guests on it.

I was really looking forward to last Friday's interview with the Saffron Girls but was very disappointed that you only showed three minutes of it. Why did you decide to cut the rest of the conversation, particularly the part where they were talking about their American tour? Please could you show the whole interview in another show soon.

Sincerely,

Jenny Philips

b) Choose a word from the box to replace the underlined words in the letter below.

| his | it | It | little boy | they | ~~its~~ | program | it |

The Cottage
Castleton
Derbyshire

May 28, 2004

Dear Sir/Madam,

I'd like to start by congratulating NBC on NBC's
(1) _its_ .... new soap opera "Buddies." This soap opera (2) .... is very realistic and the soap opera (3) .... has become my family's favorite TV soap opera (4) ....
   I'm rather confused, however, about NBC's rules on not showing violence before 8:00 at night. I was sitting with my 8-year-old son and my 8-year-old son's (5) .... friend, enjoying the story, but was extremely shocked by the murder scene, and my 8-year-old son (6) .... was very frightened by the murder scene (7) ....
   Have the regulations changed? If the regulations (8) .... have, I think parents should know.

Sincerely,

Martin Cook

module 7

Polite requests

1 **a)** Find the mistake in each of these dialogs and correct it.

1 A: Is ∧*it* all right if I close the window?
   B: Yes, go ahead.

2 A: Do you think could you turn your music down?
   B: Yes, of course. Sorry.

3 A: Would you helping me with my suitcase?
   B: I'm sorry, but I have a bad back.

4 A: Could I pass the salt please?
   B: Yes, here you are.

5 A: Can I speak to you for a minute?
   B: Yes, I'm afraid so.

6 A: Will you to get me my glasses please?
   B: Sure.

7 A: Do you mind I go now?
   B: No, that's fine. We've nearly finished.

8 A: Would you mind taking these books to the library?
   B: Yes, I would. I'm going there anyway.

9 A: Could you possible hold my umbrella for a minute?
   B: Of course.

10 A: Would you mind look after Jane for an hour?
    B: I'm afraid I can't. I'm just going out.

b) 📼 Listen to the dialogs and repeat them. Pay attention to the polite intonation.

2 **a)** Look at the following situations and complete each question so that it is polite.

1 You want to pay by credit card.
  Can *I pay by credit card* .... ?

2 You want to borrow your friend's camera.
  Do you think .... ?

3 You didn't hear what your classmate said. You want her to say it again.
  Could .... ?

4 You've written a letter in English. You want your teacher to check it.
  Would you mind .... ?

5 You can't hear what your roommate is saying because of the radio. You want him to turn it down.
  Would .... ?

6 You need five dollars. You want your colleague to lend it to you.
  Do you think .... ?

7 You haven't finished your essay. You want to give it to your teacher a day late.
  Do you mind if .... ?

8 You need to use your colleague's computer.
  Could I possibly .... ?

9 Your friend asks you to go to the movies with her. You can't tell her until tomorrow.
  Is it OK .... ?

b) 📼 Listen to the situations and complete each question politely.

You hear:

You want to pay by credit card.
Can …

You say:

Can I pay by credit card?

44

Ways of making offers

> **LOOK!**
>
> Here are some different ways of making offers:
> - *I'll **carry** that (for you) (if you like).*
> - *Shall I **carry** that (for you)?*
>
> - *Would you like me **to** carry that (for you)?*
> - *Do you want me **to** carry that (for you)?*

3 Look at these dialogs and reorder B's response to make an offer. The first word is underlined.

a A: Oh no! I've forgotten to phone Jon about the soccer game!

   B: phone – like – if – him – <u>I'll</u> – you

   I'll phone him if you like ....

e A: I really like that cassette.

   B: to – like – <u>I'll</u> – if – lend – you – it – you

   ....

   ....

f A: That's a very interesting article.

   B: you – copy – want – a – <u>Do</u> – make – you – me – to ?

   ....

   .... ?

g A: Can you give me some information about your vacations in Greece?

   B: you – our – send – to – brochure – <u>Would</u> – me – like – you ?

   ....

   .... ?

b A: I'd really love a drink.

   B: for – you – <u>Shall</u> – get – I – beer – a ?

   .... ?

c A: I can't get this videocassette recorder to work.

   B: me – want – you – try – <u>Do</u> – to ?

   .... ?

h A: Do you have the address of that electrician?

   B: down – <u>Yes</u> – I – it – for – shall – write – you ?

   ....

   .... ?

d A: Oh no, I'm going to miss my train.

   B: like – station – me – take – <u>Would</u> – to – you – to – you – the ?

   ....

   .... ?

will (instant decisions and responses)

4 a) Choose a sentence from each box to make a dialog for the situations below.

A

> The black ones look really nice, madam. Are they comfortable?
>
> How much longer are you going to be in the bathroom?
>
> Could you possibly change my flight to the evening?
>
> Is there anything good on TV tonight?
>
> Hi! Nice to see you. Come in and have a coffee.
>
> Are you ready to order?
>
> Could I speak to Mrs. Williams in the Accounts Department?
>
> I have a problem with my shower. It isn't working.

B

> Yes, very – I'll take them.
>
> OK, but I won't stay long, I can see you're busy.
>
> Yes, I'll have the fish.
>
> I'll just check the computer.
>
> I don't know – I'll have a look in the newspaper.
>
> I'll just see if she's available. Hold on, please.
>
> I'll send someone up right away. Which room is it?
>
> OK, OK, I won't be long.

1   In a shoe store.
    A: *The black ones look really nice, madam. Are they comfortable?*
    B: ....

2   In a hotel.
    A: ....
    ....
    B: ....
    ....

3   In a travel agent's.
    A: ....
    ....
    B: ....

4   Visiting a friend's house.
    A: ....
    ....
    B: ....
    ....

5   In a restaurant.
    A: ....
    B: ....

6   Phoning someone's office.
    A: ....
    ....
    B: ....
    ....

7   At home in the evening, relaxing.
    A: ....
    B: ....
    ....

8   At home in the morning, getting ready for work.
    A: ....
    ....
    B: ....

b) 🖵 Listen to the first line of each dialogue and use the prompt to respond.

You hear:

> The black ones look really nice, Madam. Are they comfortable? (take / them)

You say:

> Yes, very – I'll take them.

Jazz chant (go)

5 **a)** Complete the sentences in the jazz chant with one of the phrases from the box. Use the Present Simple in the first verse and the Past Simple in the second verse.

go swimming   go out   go to bed   go for
go away   go around   go out

On Mondays I always (1) .go out............. for a drink

And have a good long talk.

On Tuesdays I often (2) .... to my friend's

Then we (3) .... a very long walk.

On Wednesdays and Thursdays I stay at home

And (4) .... at eight.

On Fridays I sometimes (5) .... for a meal

And get back really late!

I (6) .... for most weekends

To the beach and my house by the sea.

I (7) .... and shopping on Saturdays

And on Sundays I'm home by three.

_____

On Monday John (8) .....went out...... for a drink

And had a good long talk.

On Tuesday night he (9) .... to a friend's

Then they (10) .... a very long walk.

On Wednesday and Thursday he stayed at home

And (11) .... at eight.

On Friday night he (12) .... for a meal

And got back really late.

He (13) .... for the whole weekend

To the beach and his house by the sea.

He (14) .... late on Saturday

And was dead by half past three!

b) 🔲 Listen to the jazz chant and try to say it with the cassette.

Grammar snack

Articles: making generalizations

LOOK!

When we are talking about people or things **in general**, we use a plural or an uncountable noun with **no** article:
- *I like movies and music* (**all** movies and music).
- *I like people with a sense of humor* (**all** people with a sense of humor).

Exception:
- *I hate **the** noise **of** computer games.*

For very **specific** people and things we use **the**:
- *I liked **the** movies shown in the festival.*
- ***The** people next door have a noisy dog.*

6 Complete these pairs of sentences with the correct word or phrase from the box.

exercise   the exercise   poetry   the poetry
traffic   the traffic   music   the music   people
the people   men / women   the men / the women

a 1 _Traffic_............. is one of the biggest problems in our cities.

2 You're late! Yes, ... on the way here was really bad.

b 1 What a dreadful party! .... all talked about children and .... all talked about soccer!

2 .... are physically stronger than ....

c 1 I was doing .... you showed me for 20 minutes yesterday and it really made my legs ache!

2 .... is good for you.

d 1 My husband really hates .... who chew gum all the time.

2 I thought .... at the next table were very rude to the waiter.

e 1 Grace doesn't like listening to .... when she works.

2 .... they play on that radio station is dreadful!

f 1 .... of William Wordsworth is very emotional.

2 We studied .... at school, but I haven't read much since.

Listen and read

Food from other countries

7 **a)** 📼 Sun, Maria, and Maciej are talking about meals in their countries. Read and / or listen to the texts and complete the chart.

Sun (Korean)

"Well, my mom is Korean and she told me that for breakfast people often have rice with a kind of soup that has seaweed in it, you know, the plant that grows in the sea. Then for lunch the children usually take a lunchbox with them to school with rice and kimchi in it. Kimchi's a kind of mixed vegetable dish. It has hot pepper in it. It's very common in Korea and you can have it for any meal. Then dinner is the big meal of the day. People tend to have kimchi and rice again and soup. They might also have some meat, which they cook on a hot plate on the table in front of them while they're having soup. The meat is often chicken or pork and you can put soy sauce in it."

Maria (Italian)

"Well, for breakfast of course I have cappuccino, which is coffee with a lot of milk in it, and you make it in a special machine. You can put chocolate powder on it if you like. I usually have a cornetto with it, that's a kind of sweet bread in a crescent shape, like a French croissant. And for lunch, well I usually have a sandwich because I have my main meal in the evening. For that my favorite starter is minestrone soup, which has lots of vegetables and small pasta shapes in it. Then I often have fish, or something simple like that, which is easy to cook. And then, if I want a special treat, I might have tiramisu for dessert. It's very rich and quite complicated to make. It has lots of cream in it with cake and cold coffee and liqueur. Then, of course, I have a strong espresso coffee to finish it off!"

Maciej (Polish)

"For breakfast I have a kind of open sandwich with ham and cheese or tomatoes in it. And then I often go out for lunch. A popular lunch is pierogi ruski, which are a bit like ravioli, except they have potatoes with cheese and onion in them. And then in the evening ... well in Poland most people eat a bigger meal in the evening. For example, kotlet is a traditional dish, that's meat fried in egg and breadcrumbs, often pork. I also like bigos, which is a kind of stew — sometimes you cook it for hours — it has cabbage, well sauerkraut, and different kinds of meat in it — you know, ham, bacon, sausage ... you can put dried mushrooms in it too. You have it just with bread."

	Sun	Maria	Maciej
Breakfast	*people often have rice ...*		
Lunch			
Dinner			

> **LOOK!**
> - **It has** *pepper / seaweed / ham / cabbage / mushrooms / soy beans* **in it**.
> - **You can put** *soy sauce / dried mushrooms / chili / chocolate / cheese / breadcrumbs* **in / on it**.
> - **It's a kind of** *stew / first course / dessert / cake / meat dish / sauce / pie*.
> - **It's** *easy / quick / complicated / difficult* **to make / cook**.
> - **You can have it for** *any meal / breakfast / a snack / dinner*.
> - **It's a** *traditional / light / rich / common / popular* **dish**.
> - **It's a bit like / It tastes a bit like** *ravioli / yogurt / pork*.

b) In your notebook write about a typical dish in your country / region or something you tried when you were in another country. Show it to your teacher.

Vocabulary

Food and cooking

8 Circle the word that does not belong in each group.

a   cabbage   spinach   carrot   (peach)

b   plum   melon   cauliflower   pineapple

c   prawn   lamb   pork   beef

d   mayonnaise   garlic   soy sauce   ketchup

e   saucepan   spoon   mixing bowl   frying pan

f   boil   chop   roast   bake

g   tough   overdone   delicious   burned

h   fork   corkscrew   can opener   bottle opener

i   fresh   frozen   spicy   canned

Pronunciation

Lost letters

9 **a)** In these words from module 7 one or more of the letters is not pronounced. Cross out the "lost" letter/s. Say the word aloud to see what is missing and also use the phonemic script.

1 av~~e~~rag~~e~~
/ˈævrɪdʒ/

2 restaurant
/ˈrestrənt/

3 vegetable
/ˈvedʒtəbəl/

4 considered
/kənˈsɪdərd/

5 different
/ˈdɪfrənt/

6 interestingly
/ˈɪntrəstɪŋli/

7 served
/sɜːrvd/

8 marriage
/ˈmærɪdʒ/

9 business
/ˈbɪznɪs/

b) 🖳 Listen and repeat the words. Pay attention to the stress.

Improve your writing

Sending and replying to invitations by email

10 **a)** Read these emails and find three invitations and their replies.

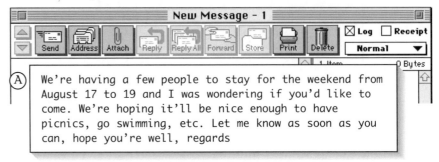

A We're having a few people to stay for the weekend from August 17 to 19 and I was wondering if you'd like to come. We're hoping it'll be nice enough to have picnics, go swimming, etc. Let me know as soon as you can, hope you're well, regards

B That's great news. Of course I'd love to come to the wedding. You'll have to send me the wedding list. Or maybe I should just buy you a surprise present?!

C Hello there! I hope you're not too busy. Could you possibly come to a meeting tomorrow at 10:30, to discuss the new book? I'm sorry it's such short notice.

D Thanks very much for the invitation. I'm afraid I've arranged to go to my parents' wedding anniversary party that weekend, so I won't be able to come. What a shame – some other time, perhaps?

E Yes, I think I can make it. I'll have to leave before 12:00 though, because I have to be on the other side of town for lunch. I hope that's all right and look forward to seeing you tomorrow.

F I know it's a strange time to be sending email, but I can't sleep! Jon and I have decided to get married and I wanted you to be the first person I invited to the wedding. It's going to be in Dublin on Saturday September 9. I'll send you a proper invitation in the mail – but I do hope you can come. If you're still awake, please reply!

1 an invitation to a meeting ...*C*.., reply ....

2 a wedding invitation ...., reply ....

3 an invitation to stay for the weekend ...., reply ....

b) Look at the e-mails again and underline useful phrases for inviting and for accepting or refusing an invitation. Now write an invitation (using email if you have it at home / work / school) and show it to your teacher.

module 8

Defining relative clauses

1 Pete is talking to Les about his vacation plans. Look at the relative pronouns in **bold** and parenthesize the ones that can be omitted.

PETE: We're thinking of going to Spain this year. You went there last year, didn't you?

LES: Yes, that's right. Actually I have some photos *(***that***)* I can show you of where we went. It was Mohacar on the south coast. A friend **whose** daughter went there last year recommended it.

PETE: Oh, someone **who** I work with has been to Mohacar. It's a very quiet area, isn't it?

LES: Yes, the thing **that** I liked most about it was the relaxing atmosphere. It's a place **where** you can forget all your problems.

PETE: How do you get there?

LES: Well, you can fly to Almeria, but that's quite expensive, or you can take any flight **that** goes to Malagar and drive east along the coast. I know several people **who** have done that. Anyway, do you want to see the photos?

2 **a)** Here are the photos from Les's vacation last year. Les is talking about the photos. Join his two sentences to make one, using a relative pronoun.

1

a   This is the apartment. We rented it …
    This is the apartment that we rented ....

b   … and these are the people. They were staying in the apartment next door.

    ....

    ....

2

a   This is the balcony. We had breakfast there every morning …

    ....

    ....

b   … and this is the beach. It was right in front of our apartment.

    ....

    ....

3

a   This is a bar. It stayed open till three in the morning …

    ....

    ....

b   … and this is the man. He owned it.

    ....

4

a   This is a fish restaurant. We had excellent meals there …

....

b   … and this is a woman. Her mother cooked wonderful paella.

....

5

a   This is one day. We went on a boat trip …

....

b   … and these are the men. We borrowed their boat.

....

6

a   This is a market. It was open every Wednesday …

....

b   … and this is me wearing a hat. I bought it there.

....

b) Look again at the sentences you have made and parenthesize the relative pronoun if it can be omitted.

Prepositions with defining relative clauses

> **LOOK!**
>
> • *She's the woman who I **spoke to**.*
> • *I'd like a balcony that I could **sit on** when it's hot.*
>
> When we use a verb or preposition in defining relative clauses, the preposition comes at the end of the clause.

3 Complete the sentences below with a preposition from the box.

on   to   in   with

a   Do you have a knife that I could cut this string *with* ?

b   Is there someone my son could talk .... about his exams?

c   Do you have something we could open this bottle .... ?

d   Angus needs a new datebook he can write all his appointments ....

e   Holly would like a radio that she could listen .... while she's in the bath.

f   Our office needs a photocopier we can do colored copies ....

g   Do you have anything I could dry these dishes .... ?

h   Is there someone we could discuss our problem .... ?

Quantifiers (*a few, a lot of,* etc.)

4 Sandra is trying to persuade Aileen to go with her to a party, but Aileen is very depressed and doesn't want to go. Match Aileen's comments with a response from Sandra.

Aileen:

a (I don't have anything to wear.

b (I have no friends.

c (I don't have much money.

d (I don't like parties where there are too many people.

e (I never have enough to talk about.

f (I have too much work to do.

g (There's no time to get ready.

Sandra:

1 (You have some time to finish it tomorrow.

2 (There's plenty of time – we don't need to be there until nine.

3 (Don't be stupid, you have lots of interesting things to say.

4 (Come on – you have loads of friends.

5 (But you have some really nice clothes.

6 (You only need enough for a taxi.

7 (Oh, but not many people have been invited tonight.

a ..5..   b ....   c ....   d ....   e ....   f ....   g ....

5 **a)** There is one mistake in each of these sentences. Find the mistake and correct it.

1 Now my father is retired he has plenty ~~of~~ time for his hobby, making model boats.

2 "Thank you all very much. You've given me a lot good ideas for the new school building. Now all we need is enough money to pay for it!"

3 There were too many of people and too much noise so Greg couldn't see or hear the president.

4 Lisbon has loads of good stores but there's not much of parking space downtown.

5 There are plenty of tickets left for the afternoon performance but no many for the evening one.

6 I think there's too much pepper in the soup but not enough of salt.

7 "Can I have plenty fruit but not much cream please."

b) Complete these sentences so that they are true for you.

1 I have too many ....
....

2 There are a lot of ....
.... in my bedroom.

3 I don't have enough ....
....

4 I don't drink much ....
....

5 I eat plenty of ....
....

6 I don't know any ....
....

7 I read loads of ....
....

8 I do a lot of ....
....

Grammar snack

Articles with countable / uncountable nouns

> **LOOK!**
> - *You have **a** very high temperature.*
> - ***The** temperature in this room is very cold.*
>
> With countable nouns we can use *a/an* or *the*.
>
> - *What ø horrible weather!*
> - ***The** weather in England is changeable.*
>
> With uncountable nouns we cannot use *a/an* but we can use *the*.

6 **a)** Put the nouns in these extracts from the *Longman Dictionary of Contemporary English* into the correct column in the chart.

sce·ne·ry /ˈsiːnəri/ *n* [U] the natural features of a particular part of a country, such as mountains, forests, deserts, etc.: *The best part of the trip was the scenery. It was fantastic.*

view[1] /vjuː/ *n* [C] what you are able to see or the possibility of seeing it: **have a good/bad/wonderful, etc. view (of)** (= be able to see a lot, very little, etc.) *We had a really good view of the whole stage from where we were sitting.*

guest house /ˈɡesthaʊs/ *n* [C] a private house where people can pay to stay and have meals

travel[2] /ˈtrævəl/ *n* [U] the act or activity of traveling: *Snow has disrupted travel in many parts of the country.*

tem·pe·ra·ture /ˈtemprətʃər/ *n* [C] a measure of how hot or cold a place or thing is: *The temperature of the water was just right for swimming.* | **a temperature of 20°/100° etc.** *Water boils at a temperature of 100° C.*

weath·er[1] /ˈweðər/ *n* [U] the temperature and other conditions such as rain and wind: **the weather** *What was the weather like on your vacation?*

mon·ey /ˈmʌni/ *n* [U] what you earn by working and what you spend in order to buy things: *The repairs will cost a lot of money.*

price[1] c/praɪs/ *n* [C] the amount of money for which something is sold, bought, or offered: *Fuel prices are rising steadily.* | **[+ of]** *Can you tell me what the price of a new window would be?*

journey[1] /ˈdʒɜːrni/ *n* [C] a trip from one place to another, especially over a long distance: *a train journey across Europe*

Countable	Uncountable
view	

b) Complete these sentences with *a/an*, *the*, or nothing (–).

1. Hello, how nice to see you. Did you have ..*a*..... good journey?
2. What .... beautiful view! You're very lucky to live here.
3. Do you have .... money I lent you?
4. Mr. Schmidt had .... bad weather on the way here.
5. There are plenty of opportunities for .... travel in this job.
6. You need to keep this liquid at .... very low temperature.
7. There's .... amazing scenery all around the hotel.
8. .... price of a ticket to Majorca has gone down.
9. My colleague Tessa stayed in .... wonderful guest house in the South of France.

Vocabulary

Formation of nouns

7 **a)** Make the verbs in the box into nouns, using the ending *-ment*, *-sion* or *-tion*. Pay attention to the spelling.

| invent equip treat compete argue permit |
| operate advertise explain produce persuade |
| decide improve discuss |

-ment	-sion	-tion
		invention

b) 🖭 Listen to the words and repeat them, paying attention to the stress.

c) Complete these sentences with the correct noun or verb from Exercise a). You may need to change the form of the verb.

1 There's been an extraordinary _improvement_ in computer design over the last 20 years.

2 I saw an .... in the newspaper for a new type of vacuum cleaner that doesn't need a bag.

3 There's a lot of .... between cellphone companies.

4 After a lot of discussion, Tom .... me to have a fax machine at home.

5 After the videocassette recorder broke down for the fifth time, Diane .... to buy a new one.

6 There's a store on the main street that sells very good sports ....

Pronunciation

/ʒ/, /ʃ/, /dʒ/, and /tʃ/

> **LOOK!**
> Compare these sounds:
> _television_ _shop_ _journey_ _teacher_
> /ʒ/ /ʃ/ /dʒ/ /tʃ/

8 a) 🖵 Listen to these words (or say them aloud) and write the correct symbol underneath.

1 invention
/ʃ/

2 research
/ /

3 decision
/ /

4 measure
/ /

5 permission
/ /

6 object
/ /

7 temperature
/ /

8 agency
/ /

9 production
/ /

10 persuasion
/ /

11 exchange
/ /

12 discussion
/ /

b) Listen again and repeat the words, paying attention to the stress.

Reading

9 Read this advertisement about cordless headphones and mark the statements below T (true) or F (false).

Want to listen to your favorite CD in the yard without disturbing the neighbors?

Try our incredible new cordless* radio frequency headphones.

These new headphones allow you to tune into your favorite radio station or TV program in complete privacy. The sound quality is excellent, and the lightweight headset is so comfortable you won't notice you're wearing it. You don't even need to be in the same room as your hi-fi or TV to enjoy your favorite sounds.

HEADPHONES

Just plug the special transmitter into your TV or stereo!

◆ The sound goes straight to your headphones and no one else will hear it!

◆ The sound signal is strong enough to go through walls, ceilings, and doors!

◆ There's a volume control on the headset itself.

◆ Relax in your yard. Listen to your favorite CD without disturbing the neighbors.

These headphones are amazing value at £34.95 incl. postage with extra sets of headphones available for just £24.95 each.

Order yours today!
Place your order on our 24-hour credit hotline.
01044-232467 – 24-hour ordering service 7 days a week.

Please allow up to 7 days for delivery. If you are not fully satisfied, we will return your money if you return the goods undamaged within 7 days.
* _cordless_ means there is no wire. You can have cordless irons and kettles.

a The headset doesn't weigh very much. ..T..

b You need to take the transmitter to the place where you want to listen. .....

c You can't use these headphones to listen to something that's in a room downstairs from where you are. .....

d If you want to turn the music up you don't need to go back to the room where the CD or television is. .....

e You have to pay extra for the postage. .....

f A second set of headphones costs less than the first one. .....

g You can ring the credit hotline at any time of the day or night. .....

h You should receive your goods after 7 days. .....

Improve your writing

Formal and informal styles

10 **a)** Look at these two letters about things that have been lost. The first is informal and the second is more formal. Complete the sentences with the correct phrase from the box.

I don't suppose you've found it / I do hope it has been found

could you mail it / I would be grateful if you could send it

let me know how much the postage is / I will of course pay for postage

I am writing to inquire whether / ~~Just writing to say~~

---

46 Broom Way

Feb. 23

Dear Andy,

(1) *Just writing to say* ....
thanks again for having us last weekend. We both had a really good time.

The only thing is I've lost one of my earrings: I know I was wearing it on Sunday, and when we got home I couldn't find it. Perhaps it fell off while I was playing with the children in the yard.

(2) .... ?

I don't know if you remember it. It's quite big, made of silver, with a blue stone set in it. The earrings are quite special to me because they were a birthday present from Peter.

If you do happen to find it,

(3) ....
to me? Obviously,

(4) ....

Anyway, I'll keep my fingers crossed!

Lots of love,
Ingrid.

---

22 Prince Avenue

Horbury

March 27, 2004

The Manager,
Sherbon Hotel
Vermont

Dear Sir/Madam,

(5) ....
you have found a camera that I left in my hotel room last weekend. I was staying in room 201 from the 21st to 23rd. I am almost certain that I left the camera in the bedside cabinet.

(6) ....
since it is a very expensive model. It is a Nikon compact, in a black leather case with a red-and-black strap.

(7) ....
by registered mail to the above address.

(8) ....

Sincerely,

I. Crompton

---

b) Imagine that you have just finished a language course in the UK, and you realize that you have left something in a classroom. Write to the school to ask about it. The address is: Success Language School, Dewbury Road, Brighton. Write the letter in your notebook and show it to your teacher.

module 9

Futures for prediction (*will, might, may,* etc.)

1 Reorder the words in these sentences. The first word is underlined.

a tonight – see – <u>I'll</u> – definitely – John
I'll definitely see John tonight ....

b probably – pass – <u>Carlos</u> – exam – English – his – won't
....
....

c so – may – us – late – don't – <u>We</u> – for – wait – be
....
....

d get – isn't – to – <u>Chris</u> – job – likely – the
....

e next – almost – <u>I'll</u> – English – year – do – here – certainly – an – course
....
....

f stay – New York – decide – in – <u>Teresa</u> – might – to
....
....

g weekend – away – probably – <u>We'll</u> – this – go
....

h lots – are – on – <u>There</u> – the – likely – beach – be – to – people – of
....
....

2 a) Rewrite these sentences so that they mean the same, using the words in parentheses.

1 Brazil is likely to win the World Cup.
Brazil *may win the World Cup* .... (*may*)

2 I don't think we'll have time to do any sightseeing.
We ....
.... (*definitely*)

3 It'll probably rain before the end of the day.
It ....
.... (*likely*)

4 Perhaps my friend Mari will be a famous actress one day.
My friend Mari ....
.... (*could*)

5 My boss is very unlikely to agree to the raise.
My boss ....
.... (*almost certainly*)

6 I think you'll recognize my sister when you see her.
You ....
.... (*probably*)

7 We probably won't get back from the theater before midnight.
We ....
.... (*likely*)

8 I'm sure that our teacher will give us a lot of homework for the weekend.
Our teacher ....
.... (*almost certainly*)

b) 🖭 Listen to the sentences and change them, using the prompts given.

You hear:
Brazil is likely to win the World Cup. (may)

You say:
Brazil may win the World Cup.

Hypothetical possibilities with *if*

3 a) Match a question from column A with an answer from column B.

A

1 If you won a lot of money, would you spend it all straightaway?

2 What would you do if someone tried to rob you in the street?

3 If your car broke down on the expressway, what would you do?

4 Would you know what to do if someone cut their arm badly?

5 If you knew a friend of yours was stealing money from his company, would you tell anyone?

6 Would you feel safe walking home alone at night in your town?

7 If someone offered you a free bungee jump, what would you do?

8 Could you ever eat raw meat?

B

a I'd probably just give him all my money and run!

b No, I definitely wouldn't – it's too dangerous.

c I think I'd probably tie something around it.

d I might do it if I was feeling brave!

e I'd go and look for a telephone.

f I might tell another friend, so that we could decide what to do.

g If I was hungry enough, yes!

h No, I'd invest some of it.

1 ...*h*... 2 .... 3 .... 4 .... 5 .... 6 ....

7 .... 8 ....

b) What would *you* do in the situations above? Write your answers below using *I'd, I wouldn't, I might, I could.*

1 ....

2 ....

3 ....

4 ....

5 ....

6 ....

7 ....

8 ....

Real and hypothetical possibilities

4 Complete the sentences in these conversations with the best form of the verb in parentheses.

a) Clare's going to have a baby. She's talking to her friend Jackie about it.

CLARE: I can't decide whether to have the baby in the hospital or not.

JACKIE: Well, I (1) *'d go*................... (go) into the hospital, especially since it's your first baby.

CLARE: Yes, you're probably right.

JACKIE: Have you decided on a name yet?

CLARE: Yes – if it (2) .... (be) a boy, we (3) .... (call) him Tom, and if it (4) .... (be) a girl, Sara.

b) Tim's mother is very worried because she's received a letter from his school, saying that he has missed a lot of lessons.

MOTHER: Why aren't you going to your classes?

TIM: Because they're so boring: I (1) .... (go) if they (2) .... (be) more interesting. And I always get bad grades.

MOTHER: Well, that's not surprising: if you (3) .... (spend) less time playing computer games and (4) .... (work) harder, you (5) .... (not / have) so many problems.

If sentences in social situations

LOOK!

We often use *if* sentences in the following ways:

• Asking for permission:
*__Would__ you mind if I **opened** the window?*
*__Would__ you mind if I **left** early today?*

• Giving advice:
*If I **were** you, **I'd** go home.*
*__You'll__ feel much better if you **have** a rest.*

• Making offers:
*__I'll__ phone her if you **like**.*
*__I'll__ get your car if you **give** me the keys.*

• Accepting invitations:
*Thank you, that **would** be very nice.*

5 **a)** Use the prompts to write complete sentences in these situations.

1 Your friend has a letter to mail. You are going out and offer to mail it.
mail it / if / want
I'll mail it if you want ....

2 It's your first evening with a host family in England and you want to telephone home. How do you ask your landlady?
all right / if / I / use / phone?

.... ?

3 Your friend is expecting a call from John, but she has to go out. What do you say?
I / take / message / if / he / phone

....

4 You're on a crowded train and you want to open the window. How do you ask the other passengers?
anyone mind / if / I / open a window?

....

5 Your car's broken down and a friend offers to take you home. What does he say?
I / give / you / lift / if / like

....

6 A friend invites you to eat in a new restaurant. What do you say?
That / be / great!

....

7 It's snowing heavily and your friend wants to drive home. How do you advise her?
I / not / drive in this weather / if / I / be / you

....

b) 🔊 Listen to the situations and respond, using the prompts.

You hear:
Your friend has a letter to mail. You are going out and you offer to mail it. I'll ...

You say:
I'll mail it if you want.

Grammar snack

Word order of adverbs (*certainly, probably, definitely*)

LOOK!

The adverb comes before the **main** verb in a positive sentence:
• *I **definitely** told her.*
• *__She's__ **probably** working too hard.*
• *__I'll__ **almost certainly** see you next week.*

Notice: When *to be* is a main verb (not an auxiliary) the adverb comes after it:
• *I was **definitely** at home at 10:30.*

The adverb comes before the **auxiliary** verb in a negative sentence:
• *I **definitely** didn't tell her.*
• *She **probably** isn't working hard enough.*
• *I **almost certainly** won't see you next week.*

6 Rewrite these sentences, putting the adverb in parentheses into the correct position.

a The waitress has made a mistake with the check. (*definitely*)
The waitress has definitely made a mistake with the check

b My aunt won't hear the phone. (*almost certainly*)

....

c Don't ask Nick about the lecture: he wasn't listening. (*probably*)

....

d It's 11:00 ... they've missed their train. (*almost certainly*)

....

e Stephen doesn't smoke. (*definitely*)

....

f Don't call Kate, she isn't home yet. (*probably*)

....

g Jos didn't take the money: he was with me all day. (*definitely*)

....

Vocabulary

Money verbs and prepositions

7 **a)** Read these paragraphs about what people do with money, and circle the correct preposition.

Ⓐ

"I don't know why my daughter wastes money (1) by / (on) unnecessary things like magazines and makeup. If she was more careful and put a little money (2) into / for the bank every month, she could save up (3) for / on something really nice, like a new CD player."

Ⓑ

"I'm really fed up with my boyfriend: he never has any money. He doesn't pay (4) on / for drinks or a meal when we go out, and you can see that he never spends any money (5) in / on clothes! In fact, I don't think I've ever seen him take any money (6) off / out of the bank."

Ⓒ

"My grandma is really old-fashioned: she hates banks. When she goes shopping she always pays (7) on / in cash: she thinks that if you pay (8) with / by check or credit card, it's not "real" money. She has lots of money, though, and I'm always telling her to invest it (9) in / into some kind of business, instead of keeping it under the mattress."

b) Complete these sentences with the best form of a verb from the box and / or the correct preposition.

| waste   invest   ~~put~~   take   pay (x 3) |
| save up   spend |

1 Bob: Each month I ..*put*.......... about a quarter of my salary ..*into*... the bank, because I'm ....
.... a vacation in the Bahamas and I'm really trying not to ....
money .... stupid things like beer and lottery tickets.

2 Sheila: I don't carry much cash around with me. When I go shopping for food, I usually .... check.

3 Katie: My mom .... all my clothes, and she gives me some money every week to .... candy and magazines.

4 Paul: I don't like .... money .... an ATM when it's late at night. I know someone who was robbed while he was doing that.

5 Jack: I do a lot of small building jobs for people, so I prefer it if they ....
me .... cash. I suppose about three quarters of my customers do this.

6 Maria: Well, my souvenir store's doing very well at the moment, so I'm planning to .... two thirds of the profits .... another store.

Improve your writing

Opening a bank account

If you go to stay in an English-speaking country for more than a few months you may want to open a bank account.

Application to open a checking account

PLEASE COMPLETE IN BLOCK CAPITALS

Title: .... Family name: ....

First name(s): ....

Date of birth: ....

Nationality: ....

Address: ....

....

....

Zip code: ....

Tel: Home No. .... Work No. ....

Marital status: .... Number of dependent children: ....

Where do you live? With parents ❑ Alone ❑

With partner ❑ Other ❑

Previous address: ....

....

....

Zip code: ....

When did you move to your current address?

Month .... Year ....

What type of other bank or savings and loan association accounts do you hold?

Checking ❑ Savings ❑ Other ❑

How many of each of the following payment cards do you have?

Credit card ❑ Store cards ❑ Debit cards ❑

Employment status (e.g. full-time / part-time / student): ....

Job title (e.g. sales clerk): ....

Employer's name and address / Place of study: ....

....

....

Zip code: ....

When did you start working for your current employer / start your course of study? Month .... Year ....

Mother's maiden name: ....

(This personal information may be required as identification for security measures only.)

Signature ....

Date ....

---

8 a) Look at the vocabulary from the form and match each word or phrase (1–9) with a definition / example (a–i).

1	title	a	single – married – divorced
2	marital status	b	You can use this card to buy something and pay at the end of the month.
3	mother's maiden name	c	You use this account for saving.
4	checking account	d	Your mother's family name before she was married.
5	savings account	e	Mrs. – Mr. – Ms. – Miss
6	zip code:	f	You can use this card to buy things at a particular store, e.g. a department store.
7	store card	g	You can take money from this account whenever you like.
8	credit card	h	You can use this card in the same way as a check. The money is taken directly from your bank account.
9	debit card	i	A group of five or nine numbers that are added to an address to help the delivery of mail.

1 ...e...   2 ....   3 ....   4 ....   5 ....   6.......   7 ....
8 ....   9 ....

b) You have come to the UK for a year. Decide whether you have come to:

- work for FBT Inc. as a trainee manager. The company's office is at: 7 Grosvenor Place, London WC1 2RP.

- take an English course. The address of the school is: International English, 40 Baker Street, London NW1.
  You have rented an apartment at this address: Apartment 3, 2 Croxted Road, London SE14 2PQ.
  Phone number: 0181-629-4731.
  Now complete the bank application form and ask your teacher to check it.

Listen and read

Lottery winners

9 a) Which of these things do you expect people to do if they win a lottery "jackpot" (the biggest prize)?

1 give up their job / stay in the same job?
2 stay in their old home / buy a new home?
3 give away money to their family / keep all the money for themselves?
4 eat in expensive restaurants / almost never go out?

b) 🖳 Read and / or listen to this text about Bert Dunstan and mark the statements below *T* (True) or *F* (False).

TWO YEARS AGO Bert Dunstan won £12,000,000 in the National Lottery. Today he is dead. The 53-year-old factory worker was found lying lifeless on the couch at his home last weekend.

When Bert won his fortune, he immediately gave up his £200-a-week job at the local chocolate factory and bought a luxurious new house. However, he did not immediately head for the sun on a Caribbean vacation or an around-the-world cruise, as others have done; instead, he packed his family of seven into one of his new cars and took them camping in Scotland.

Bert always liked his food and, instead of giving his only daughter, Sally, part of his winnings, he employed her as a full-time cook on a salary of £500 a week. "I used to cook him three big meals every day: burgers, steak, and fries were his favorites." But Sally doesn't think Bert died through overeating: "He just seemed to lose interest in life."

Chloe Godwin, a psychologist who specializes in the effects that winning a large amount of money can have on people, says, "For some people the most terrible thing that can happen to them is change. This is why people have problems when they get married or pass exams. It's nice to win a few thousand pounds, but you shouldn't have so much that you move too far away from the life you have."

Certainly other lottery winners have had their problems: one of them left the country because of the publicity and because her family was fighting over the money. Another left his wife of 40 years and gave her nothing – the ticket was in *his* name, after all!

Losing can be just as bad, though: Freddie McMahon actually went mad when a group of people at his office won the jackpot – and he had refused to join them the week before.

So, whichever way you look at it, you just can't win!

1 Bert died two years after winning the lottery. ..*T*..
2 He spent some of the money on a new car. .....
3 He only gave his daughter £500. .....
4 Sally thinks that Bert ate himself to death. .....
5 The psychologist says that people find it very difficult when they have big changes in their lives. .....
6 One person left the country partly because of her relatives. .....
7 A husband and wife bought a winning lottery ticket together and then he left her. .....
8 Freddie McMahon went mad over a lottery ticket. .....

Pronunciation

/ʌ/

> **LOOK!**
> The sound /ʌ/ can be spelled in different ways:
> d<u>o</u>ne   l<u>u</u>nch   t<u>ou</u>gh
> /ʌ/   /ʌ/   /ʌ/

10 a) Find and underline nine words in the box that contain /ʌ/.

<u>public</u>	stomach	burn
luxury	cough	rough
through	money	woman
push	enough	budget
tongue	encourage	huge

b) 🖳 Listen to the words and repeat them.

c) Complete these sentences with one of the words.

1 There's a .*public*............ telephone over there.

2 Have you had .... cake?

3 Ow! I've bitten my .... !

4 My mother tried to .... me to apply for the job.

5 Don't go swimming today because the sea's too ....

6 Ian hit me in the ....

7 Could you lend me some .... ?

8 Many years ago, chocolate used to be a ....

9 Has your department planned its .... for next year?

module 10

Past Perfect or Past Simple

1 Complete these sentences with the best form of the verb in parentheses (in each sentence one verb should be in the Past Perfect and the other(s) in the Past Simple).

a When the movie ...*started*................ (*start*) Beth realized she *'d seen*.................... (*see*) it before.

b I .... (*be*) surprised to find that Mr. Cole .... (*leave*) the city the day before.

c Helen .... (*feel*) much better after she .... (*have*) a good sleep.

d The rain .... (*stop*) by the time we .... (*get*) to the beach.

e Melissa .... (*be*) angry because her brother .... (*eat*) all the chocolates.

f When Julia .... (*meet*) Scott she .... (*not realize*) he .... (*be married*) before.

g Geoff .... (*not see*) his parents for fifteen years so he .... (*feel*) rather nervous at the airport.

h The jazz singer .... (*sing*) an old blues song that I .... (*never hear*) before.

i When I .... (*write*) the letter I .... (*mail*) it right away.

j Before Marti .... (*become*) Mrs. Stephens's personal assistant she .... (*work*) as a receptionist.

k After Sarah .... (*know*) Alan for a few months he .... (*ask*) her to have dinner with him.

Present Perfect or Past Perfect

2 a) Check (✔) the correct ending for each of these sentences.

1 Greg felt terrified because
 a he's never flown before.
 b he'd never flown before. ✔

2 How's Susan?
 a I haven't seen her for ages.
 b I hadn't seen her for ages.

3 The group Just Girls are breaking up and
 a they've only been together for 3 months.
 b they'd only been together for 3 months.

4 We were all very tired because
 a we've just traveled back from Florida.
 b we'd just traveled back from Florida.

5 It's the best restaurant
 a I've ever been to.
 b I'd ever been to.

6 The whole country was in shock because
 a the President has died.
 b the President had died.

7 It was the first time Juventus
 a have lost a game.
 b had lost a game.

8 What's the matter?
 a You've been depressed all week.
 b You'd been depressed all week.

b) Complete these sentences with your own ideas (use either the Present Perfect or the Past Perfect).

1 This is the best meal ....

2 It was the first time ....

3 Dave was surprised because ....
....

4 I'm not very hungry because ....
....

5 Sue played really badly because ....
....

6 The room was very cold because ....
....

63

Reported statements

3 **a)** Complete the sentences with a statement from the speech bubbles. Sometimes there are two possibilities.

Ten people have been killed in a bomb attack.

I practiced eight hours every day.

The world is flat.

I've just got married.

Stephen's doing very well in math.

You can be anything you want to be!

I'm sure I heard somebody in the yard, Inspector.

People in Brazil use the Internet more than anyone.

It'll rain overnight.

1 When I interviewed Mrs. Taylor she said that *she was sure she'd heard somebody in the yard* .

2 On the weather forecast last night they said ....
....

3 Stephen's teacher told us ....
....

4 When I was young my father told me ....
....

5 They said on the news this morning that ....
....

6 Six hundred years ago people thought that ....
....

7 I've just been reading an article in *Computer Monthly*, which said that ....
....

8 My ex-boyfriend sent me a letter saying that ....
....

9 Wayne Rider, the new tennis star, said that when he was young ....
....

b) 📼 Listen to some statements and use the prompts to report them.

You hear:
I'm tired. Jack said ...

You say:
Jack said he was tired.

Reported questions

4 **a)** Clare has just arrived at San Francisco airport, where her friend Josh is meeting her. Clare took a long time to go through customs. Report the questions that she was asked.

What happened? Why are you so late?

Oh, I had a terrible time in customs. They asked me so many questions ...

1 Where are you from?
He asked me where I was from ....

2 Are you traveling alone?
....

3 Did you pack your suitcases yourself?
....

4 Do you have any hand luggage?
....

5 Did you get off the plane at the stopover in Amsterdam?
....
....

6 How long will you be in the country?
....

7 Where are you going to stay?
....

8 How much money have you brought with you?
....

b) 📼 Listen to the questions and report them.

You hear:
Where are you from?

You say:
He asked me where I was from.

say and *tell*

> **LOOK!**
> - *I **told** to Fran that I'd be late.*
>   *tell + object*
> - *I **said** Fran I'd be late.*
>   *say without object*
> - *I **said** to Fran that I'd be late.*
>   *say + to + object*

5 Five of these sentences have mistakes. Find the mistakes and correct them.

a   Sorry, what did you ~~tell~~ *say*?

b   The press report said the President had been in an accident.

c   Matthew hasn't told his boss that he's leaving yet.

d   Roseanne's father said her she should be more polite.

e   Danny told he was going to the USA.

f   Tell to your brother that you're sorry.

g   Mr. Stuart said a lot of interesting things about the new plans.

h   Could you say me your name again, please.

Vocabulary

Weather phrases

6 a) Match a weather phrase from column A with a result from column B.

A		B	
1	It was a dark, stormy night	a	so I put the laundry out to dry.
2	There was thick fog	b	so old Mrs. Lampeter had to walk carefully.
3	There was a very strong wind	c	so I hurried home from work and stayed in front of the fire.
4	The snow was a meter deep	d	so everybody put on extra sweaters and scarves.
5	The streets were very slippery	e	so we decided not to go sailing.
6	It was freezing cold	f	and the grass was white and sparkling in the sun.
7	It was pouring with rain	g	so Bud had to drive slowly because he couldn't see.
8	There was a warm breeze	h	so we had to clear the path before we could go out.
9	It was a boiling hot day	i	and the children got very wet.
10	It was a clear, frosty morning	j	so they closed the car windows and turned on the air conditioning.

1 ..*c*..   2 ....   3 ....   4 ....   5 ....
6 ....   7 ....   8 ....   9 ....   10 ....

b) Now cover the phrases (1–10) and test yourself. Look at the sentences below and complete each one with the missing word.

1 It was *freezing* cold.

2 There was a very .... wind.

3 There was .... fog.

4 It was a .... hot day.

5 The streets were very ....

6 It was a dark, ... night.

7 It was .... with rain.

8 It was a clear, ... morning.

9 The snow was a meter ....

10 There was a warm ....

Listen and read

Sherlock Holmes

In all the stories about the famous detective Sherlock Holmes, the storyteller is his assistant, Dr. Watson. Inspector Lestrade is a detective from Scotland Yard.

7 a) 📼 Read and / or listen to this extract from "The Six Busts of Napoleon" and answer the questions.

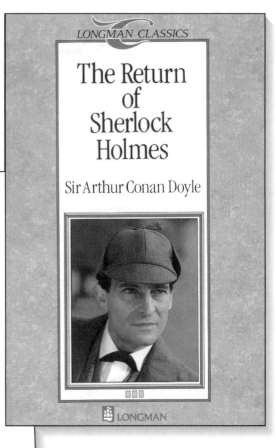

LONGMAN CLASSICS

The Return of Sherlock Holmes

Sir Arthur Conan Doyle

LONGMAN

Lestrade and I woke up at half past ten. Holmes was waiting for us. He told me to bring my gun and I saw him pick up his favourite strong walking stick before we left the house.

We quickly drove to Chiswick, and Holmes took us to a large house in a dark street. I thought that the people inside must have already gone to bed because the house was so dark and quiet.

"I'm glad it's not raining," said Holmes quietly. "We may have to wait a long time. We mustn't smoke and we must be very quiet, but I hope we are going to discover something tonight."

We waited for five minutes but we didn't have to wait much longer. The garden gate suddenly opened and a man ran quickly down the garden path towards the house. It was so dark and he moved so quickly that it was impossible to see his face. He disappeared into the darkness and we waited in silence.

The next thing we heard was the sound of a window opening very slowly, then we saw a small light inside the front room of the house.

"Let's go to the open window, then we can catch him as he comes out," said Lestrade.

But before we could move, the man had come outside again. In the light we could see that he had something white under his arm. He looked around to see if anyone was watching him. Then there was a sudden crash as he broke the thing against the wall. He was so busy that he didn't see the three of us coming towards him. Holmes jumped on his back and he fell to the ground heavily. Lestrade and I quickly ran to help Holmes. I had my gun ready and soon it was impossible for the man to escape.

1 Does it take place during the day or night?

2 How many people are involved in this part of the story?

b) Listen and / or read again and mark these statements *T* (true) or *F* (false).

1 Holmes and Watson know the situation will be dangerous. ..*T*.

2 They got wet while they waited. .....

3 A man comes out of the house after five minutes. .....

4 Watson recognizes the man. .....

5 The man climbs into the house through a window. .....

6 The man steals something from the house, then breaks it. .....

7 The man attacks Sherlock Holmes. .....

Pronunciation

Connected speech: links between words

> **LOOK!**
>
> Here is an extract from the Sherlock Holmes story "The Six Busts of Napoleon." Notice how we link some words: **Lestrade and I**
>
> consonant + vowel
>
> "Lestrade and I woke up at half past ten. Holmes was waiting for us. He told me to bring my gun and I saw him pick up his favourite strong walking stick before we left the house."

8 a) Mark the links between words in this paragraph from the Sherlock Holmes story.

> But before we could move, the man had come outside again. In the light we could see that he had something white under his arm. He looked around to see if anyone was watching him. Then there was a sudden crash as he broke the thing against the wall. He was so busy that he didn't see the three of us coming towards him. Holmes jumped on his back and he fell to the ground heavily. Lestrade and I quickly ran to help Holmes. I had my gun ready and soon it was impossible for the man to escape.

b) 🔊 Listen to the paragraph and repeat each phrase, giving special attention to the links.

Grammar snack

Definite article for shared knowledge

> **LOOK!**
>
> We use *the* when it is clear to the reader or listener which person or thing we are talking about:
>
> - *"Are you coming to **the** bar?"*
>   (The speaker and the listener both know which bar.)
> - *"There's **a** nice bar about 10 minutes away."*
>   (The listener doesn't know the bar.)
> - *"Who's that at **the** door?"*
>   (The speaker and the listener know that this means the front door of the building they are in.)
> - *"I heard **a** door open."*
>   (The speaker doesn't know which door.)

9 Here is the beginning of a Sherlock Holmes story, "The Golden Glasses." Dr. Watson is telling the story. Complete the sentences with *a / an* or *the*.

> It was (1) ...*a*..... very stormy night near the end of November. Sherlock Holmes and I were reading by (2) .... fire. It was late, and most people were in bed. There was no one outside in (3) .... street.
>
> Holmes put down his book, and said, "I'm glad that we don't have to go out tonight, Watson."
>
> "So am I," I replied.
>
> Just then we heard (4) .... carriage stop outside (5) .... house. Someone was getting out. I went to (6) .... window and looked outside.
>
> "Someone is coming here," I said.
>
> "I wonder who it is," Holmes answered.
>
> Very soon we knew who our visitor was. It was (7) .... young detective from Scotland Yard. Holmes and I had helped him with some cases in the past.
>
> "Come and sit down by (8) .... fire," said Holmes. "It's (9) .... very cold, wet night. I think you must have (10) .... interesting case for me!"

Improve your writing

Time expressions for telling stories

10 **a)** Sheila keeps a diary about what happens to her each day. Read these extracts about how she met Gregory, a Russian man studying English. Complete the sentences with a suitable word or phrase from the box. (You will need to use some of them more than once.)

after   afterwards   during   for   until   when
while   in the end   at first

Saturday, September 9

Sue's party – I felt a bit shy (1) .at first............ because I didn't know anyone. Then Sue introduced me to one of her students, a man called Gregory, from Moscow. I chatted to him quite a lot – his English is really good!

Tuesday, September 12

I went to the library and (2) .... I was looking for a book I saw Gregory, the guy from Sue's party. He was doing his English homework and (3) .... he saw me, he asked me if I could help him with some words he didn't know. I sat down with him (4) .... a few minutes and helped him finish the exercises. (5) ...., he insisted on buying me a coffee, and we chatted (6) .... hours – (7) .... the coffee shop shut, in fact!

Wednesday, September 13

Gregory phoned and asked me to go to a concert with him (8) .... work tomorrow night. (9) .... I wasn't sure, because of having to get up early the next day, but Gregory explained that it was a famous Russian pianist, so (10) .... I said I'd go.

Thursday, September 14

We had a great evening. The music was fantastic and I really enjoyed being with Gregory. (11) .... the intermission we met some of G's friends, and (12) .... we all went to a wine bar downtown. G. brought me home and we've arranged to meet again at the weekend. I'm really looking forward to seeing him again ...

LOOK!

These pairs of time expressions can be easily confused:

- **After** the lesson, we went for a drink.
  After + noun

- **Afterwards**, we took a taxi home.
  Afterwards + clause

- It was a terrible day. **First** I missed the bus, then I spilled coffee all over my skirt.
  First is used to show the order of events or instructions.

- I hated my boss **at first**, but now we get along well.
  At first refers to a point of time before another point of time.

- **At the end** of the movie she died.
  At the end = when something finishes.

- **In the end** I agreed to help them.
  In the end = finally, after a period of time.

b) Complete these sentences with a word or phrase from the box.

after   in the end   first   at the end   at first
afterwards

1 *At the end*........ of the concert, Liam took his shirt off and threw it into the audience.

2 .... I pulled the injured man out of the car and then I called the ambulance.

3 I thought Phil was joking .... but then I realized he was serious.

4 I said goodbye and put the phone down. ...., I remembered something I'd forgotten to say.

5 Sara didn't really want to come on vacation with us, but .... she agreed to come.

6 .... the long journey to my grandparents' house, I just wanted to go to bed.

module 11

Obligation and permission

1 Complete these sentences with a word or phrase from the box.

> should shouldn't can can't must mustn't
> ought ~~have~~ don't have are allowed
> aren't allowed

a You ....*have*.......... to leave your keys at the reception desk when you go out of the hotel.

b I think people .... spend more time with their families and less time at work.

c Passengers .... to walk around the plane when it is taking off.

d Candidates .... to take a dictionary into the exam, but they can't take in a grammar book.

e You .... buy alcohol in a bar unless you're over 21.

f You look really tired. I think you .... to take a day off.

g Monday's a holiday so we .... to go to school until Tuesday.

h You .... ride a bicycle on the expressway – it's very dangerous.

i Guests .... have breakfast any time between 7:00 and 9:00 a.m.

j I know I .... really smoke so much, but it helps me to relax.

k You .... sign your name in this book when you enter or leave the building.

2 Here are the answers to some questions about rules. First decide if they are about a language class (LC), a library (LIB), or a sports club (SC) and then use the prompts to make complete questions.

a You can borrow up to three books at a time. _LIB_..
   How many books / allowed / at a time?
   How many books am I allowed to borrow at a time ?

b Yes, you can book up to two days in advance. ....
   Can / aerobics classes / in advance?
   .... ?

c You're allowed to keep them for three weeks. ....
   How long / allowed / books?
   .... ?

d Yes, first you take a short written test, then there's an interview with a teacher. ....
   I / have to / test?
   .... ?

e Yes, bring a passport-sized photo for your membership card. ....
   Should / a photo?
   .... ?

f No, you don't have to – you can join for just six months if you like. ....
   I / have to / a whole year?
   .... ?

g Well, if you miss too many, you won't get a certificate at the end of the course. ....
   How many classes / allowed?
   .... ?

Obligation and permission in the past

3 Reorder the words in these conversations. The first word is underlined.

a) Kim and Pieter are talking about a math exam.

KIM: exam – to – calculator – <u>Were</u> – a – allowed – the – take – into – you ?

Were you allowed to take a calculator into the exam?

PIETER: weren't – <u>No</u> – we

....

KIM: did – answer – many – have – <u>How</u> – questions – to – you ?

....

....

PIETER: three – <u>We</u> – do – in – had – hours – twenty – to

....

b) Patrizia and Italo are talking about a summer camp.

PATRIZIA: up – allowed – you – late – to – <u>Were</u> – stay ?

.... ?

ITALO: campfire – we – by – midnight – <u>Yeah</u> – until – sit – the – could

....

....

PATRIZIA: get – early – you – up – <u>Did</u> – to – have ?

.... ?

ITALO: to – nine – we – <u>No</u> – up – didn't – until – get – have

....

c) Mona is talking to Vanessa about Vanessa's daughter, Françoise.

MONA: America – a – <u>Did</u> – have – Françoise – time – in – good ?

....

.... ?

VANESSA: six – week – to – she – work – <u>No</u> – a – days – had

....

....

MONA: terrible – <u>That's</u> !

.... !

VANESSA: allowed – us – to – wasn't – she – phone – <u>And</u>

....

4 These people are talking about their lives when they were about fourteen. Change the sentences (if necessary) so that they are true for you.

a MARIA: I had to wear white gloves and a hat to school.

I didn't have to wear gloves or a hat ....

b JOHN: I couldn't stay up after 8:00 p.m. during the week.

....

c LISBETH: We were allowed to wear whatever we wanted at school.

....

d PAOLO: I had to go to church twice on Sundays.

....

e ANNA: I could go out to play with my friends whenever I wanted to.

....

f JANE: We weren't allowed to speak in the corridors at school.

....

g JUDIT: We could call our teachers by their first names.

....

h MARK: I was allowed to watch any TV programs I wanted.

....

must and have to

5 Complete these sentences with a word or phrase from the box.

> must   mustn't (x2)   have to   don't have to (x2)
> had to   didn't have to

a You ....*mustn't*.......... smoke in the library.

b It's free to get in: you .... pay.

c I missed my train and I .... wait half an hour for the next one.

d It's not a direct flight to New Zealand: you .... change planes at Bangkok.

e There were only two people in front of me in the line so I .... wait long.

f Don't cry, Jessica – you .... play with Jon if you don't want to.

g Children .... walk on the railroad line.

h I .... remember to mail this letter.

make and *let*

> Let (permission)
>
> • *My sister **lets her children do** whatever they like.*
>   (*let* + object + base form)
>   = My sister allows her children to do whatever they like.
>
> Make (obligation)
>
> • *My mother **makes me clean** my room every week.*
>   (*make* + object + base form)
>   = I have to clean my room every week (my mother tells me to do it).

LOOK!

6 Match a sentence from column A with one from column B and complete the sentences with the best form of *let* or *make*.

A

a My boss was very understanding when my mother was ill.

b The doctor was very patient.

c Our teacher is really strict.

d Lucy was delayed at the airport.

e Don and Rita were very generous.

f There's a really good documentary on TV tonight.

g That woman in the sales department is very difficult to please.

B

1 The customs officer .... her open her suitcase.

2 She .... me write two of my reports again.

3 Don't .... me forget to videotape it.

4 He .... us work very hard.

5 He .*let*.... me have two days off work.

6 She .... me talk about all my problems.

7 They .... us spend a week in their house in the mountains.

a ..*5*..   b ....   c ....   d ....   e ....   f ....   g ....

Spelling and pronunciation

School / university subjects

7 a) Each of the subjects in the box has a spelling mistake. Correct the mistake.

> mathmatics   giography   biologie   fisics   cemistry   histery
>
> langauges   litterature   information tecnology   sosciology
>
> sychology   filosophy   phisical education   midia studies
>
> religous studies   economicks

b) 🔲 Listen to the words and mark the stressed syllables ● and the unstressed syllables ○,

e.g. ma·the·ma·tics. (○ ●○)

c) Complete these sentences so that they are true for you.

1 My favorite subject is / was

....

because ....

....

2 I am / was very good at

....

3 I hate / hated

....

because ....

....

4 I am / was hopeless at

....

5 I find / found

.... very difficult.

6 .... is / was very boring.

7 I like / liked

.... but I'm not / I wasn't very good at it.

8 I find / found

.... really interesting.

Vocabulary

Transportation: noun + noun

8 Pair a noun from box A with a noun from box B and complete the sentences.

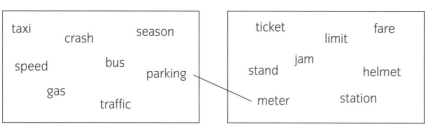

A

taxi   crash   season
speed   bus   parking
gas   traffic

B

ticket   fare
limit
jam
stand   helmet
meter   station

a   I put $2 in the *parking... meter*......, so we can leave the car here until 5:30.

b   I'm sorry I'm late. There was a terrible .... near the soccer ground, because of all the people coming out of the game.

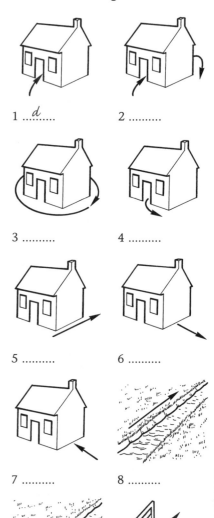

c   The last bus has gone, but there's a .... in the next street: it won't cost much to go to your hotel.

d   If you're going to take the train to work every day, it's cheaper to buy a ....

e   I think we should stop at the next .... and fill the car up for the journey.

f   It's very dangerous to ride a motorbike without a ....

g   Don't drive so fast! The ....'s 60 mph on this road.

h   I have only got a $20 bill: could you lend me 90¢ for my .... ?

Grammar snack

Prepositions of movement

9 **a)** Look at the arrow in the pictures (1–10). Choose one of the phrases (a–j) below to say where the arrow goes.

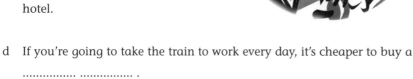

1 *d*........   2 ....

3 ....   4 ....

5 ....   6 ....

7 ....   8 ....

9 ....   10 ....

a   along the river
b   through the gate
c   past the house
d   into the house
e   through the house
f   across the river
g   toward the house
h   out of the house
i   around the house
j   away from the house

b) Look at this plan of an airport terminal and complete the sentences in the directions below with a suitable preposition.

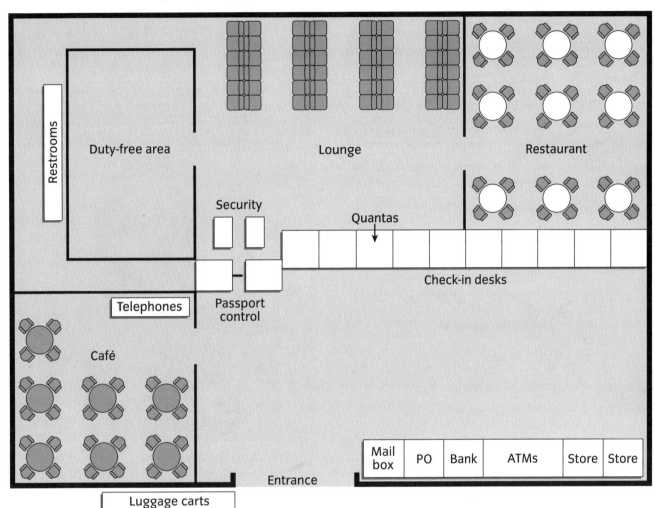

1   (At the entrance) Are there any ATMs here?

Yes, you go ......*past*....... the post office and bank and they're just on the right.

2   (At the ATM) Is there anywhere I can mail this letter?

If you go .... the entrance, there's a mailbox next to the Post Office.

3   (At the mailbox) Excuse me, where can I get a luggage cart?

Go .... the terminal building and they're just outside on your right.

4   (At the luggage cart area) Could you tell me where the Quantas check-in desk is, please?

Yes. Go .... the entrance and you'll see lots of check-in desks in front of you. Quantas is the third one.

5   (At the Quantas check-in desk) Where are the telephones, please?

Go .... passport control and .... the café: they're just on your right.

6   (In the café) Is there anywhere to get something to eat in the departure lounge?

Yes, there's quite a big restaurant. When you've gone .... passport control and security, go .... the lounge and you'll see it.

7   (In the restaurant) Could you tell me where the restrooms are?

Yes, go .... the back of the duty-free area over there, and you'll see them.

Grammar snack

-ing forms as nouns

> **LOOK!**
>
> • **It's dangerous** to **drive** when you're tired.
>
> • **Driving** when you're tired **is dangerous**.
>
> Notice: *Driving* is now a noun, and is the subject of the sentence.

10 Look at the sentences below and rewrite them using an -ing form.

a   It's compulsory to wear a seatbelt in a car.

Wearing a seatbelt in a car is compulsory .

b   It's quite easy to buy a gun.

....

c   It's possible to park on the sidewalk.

....

d   It's forbidden to wear shorts in church.

....

e   It's common to live with your parents until you get married.

....

f   It's difficult to get a divorce.

....

g   It's not a good idea to walk alone at night.

....

h   It's permitted to get married at the age of 14.

....

i   It isn't compulsory to wear a crash helmet on a motorbike.

....

j   It is illegal to buy drugs.

....

Improve your writing

Linking words

11 Read the text and circle the correct linking word.

Surrogate Mothers:
IS THE PRICE TOO HIGH?

Nowadays science has made it possible for a couple who can't have children to pay a woman to have their baby for them. These "surrogate" mothers sign a contract promising to give the baby to the couple as soon as it is born, in return for a large sum of money. (1) *However*/ *Also*, this business arrangement does not always work well in practice and, (2) *despite this / as a result*, there have been a number of "horror stories" in the newspapers recently.

People have strong feelings on both sides. Some say that it is every woman's right to have a child. (3) *Although / What is more*, a surrogate mother can often save an unhappy marriage and make some money for herself. (4) *Therefore / Despite this*, many people are against this practice. They say that (5) *although / besides* they understand the heartache of a childless woman, having a baby is not an automatic right. They feel the whole thing is completely unnatural and (6) *for this reason / also* should not be allowed. (7) *Besides / However*, they ask what will happen to the child when he or she is old enough to know the truth. This could have a terrible effect on their mental and emotional development. I feel that this last point is particularly important and (8) *therefore / what is more*, I tend to agree that surrogacy is wrong, or at least that there should be stricter rules about it.

could have / should have / would have

1 Look at the pictures and match them to the captions below.

a "Oh well, they wouldn't have had room for my luggage, anyway."

b "What do you mean, you gave him your candies? I'd have hit him."

c "Darling, you could have hurt yourself."

d "Oh well, it's not too bad – we could have lost everything."

e "I knew I shouldn't have gone to that hairdresser." "You should have told me your boss was a vegetarian."

e
....   2 ....   3 ....   4 ....   5 ....   6 ....

2 Complete these sentences with a phrase from the box, and the best form of the verb in parentheses.

> could have (x2)   couldn't have   should have (x2)
> shouldn't have   would have (x2)   wouldn't have

a Oh no, I've forgotten Marcel's address. I knew I *should have written* .... (*write*) it down.

b Why didn't you buy them that picture? I'm sure they .... (*like*) it.

c We did our best to catch the train: we .... (*run*) any faster.

d You .... (*listen*) to Paul. You know he has some stupid ideas.

e I like Kristin's new motorbike, but I .... (*buy*) a bigger one.

f Look where you're going – we were really close to that car. We .... (*have*) an accident.

g You were right not to tell her the truth about Brian: she .... (*believe*) you, anyway.

h Rupert .... (*be*) a great pianist, but he didn't practice enough.

i The room was a terrible mess when the men had finished painting it. I .... (*do*) it myself.

3 🔊 Listen to these sentences and repeat what you hear (circle the correct phrase).

a *You shouldn't walk / (You shouldn't have walked)* home so late at night.

b *We could invite / We could have invited* our teacher to the picnic on Saturday.

c Do you still have a headache? *You should take / You should have taken* an aspirin.

d I'm glad you bought a cake. *I wouldn't have / I wouldn't have had* time to make one.

e Has Jon really gone running in this rain? *I'd stay / I'd have stayed* at home.

f Mom and I waited for nearly an hour. *We couldn't wait / We couldn't have waited* any longer.

Past sentences with *if*

4 Look at these half sentences and match a first half from column A with a second half from column B.

A

a If I hadn't lost my passport

b If Sara and I had stayed longer in Paris

c If we'd booked our theater tickets in advance

d If Greta hadn't spent $10,000 on a new car

e If Malcolm had stopped smoking

f If my uncle lived near the airport

g If it hadn't rained

h If you hadn't taken so long to get ready

B

1 she'd have enough money to pay her rent.

2 I'd have stayed at his house on my way to Germany.

3 I'd be on the plane to Tunisia.

4 we wouldn't have had to stand in line outside.

5 we could have taken the children to the zoo.

6 we wouldn't have missed our bus.

7 he wouldn't have such a terrible cough.

8 we'd have visited Euro Disney.

a ..*3*.. b .... c .... d .... e .... f .... g .... h ....

5 Rewrite the following sentences so that they mean the same, using a past sentence with *if*.

a Kristin moved to San Francisco and that's how she met Ralph.
Kristin *wouldn't have met Ralph if she hadn't moved to San Francisco* .

b You didn't wear a sweater. That's why you're cold.
If you ....

c Josh was very tired and so he lost his temper.
Josh ....
....

d Sam didn't do his homework, so he doesn't know the answer.
If Sam ....
....

e My hair looks terrible. That's because I didn't go to my usual hairdresser.
If I ....
....

f I don't have a very well-paid job because I haven't done a computer course.
If I'd ....
....

g Alice wasn't at home last night. That's why she didn't get your message.
Alice ....
....

h The store manager knew Ruth's father. That's why he gave her the job.
If the store manager ....
....

6 Complete these sentences with your own ideas.

a If you'd been more careful doing the dishes ....
....
....
....

b If I'd put the correct stamp on the letter ....
....
....
....

c If we'd put more salt and pepper on the food ....
....
....
....

d If the weather had been better last weekend ....
....
....
....

e If my mother hadn't lent me some money ....
....
....
....

Grammar snack

Verb + object + infinitive

> **LOOK!**
>
> - *The doctor **told me to drink** more water.*
>   (*tell* + object + infinitive)
> - *The doctor **told me not to drink** so much beer.*
>   (*tell* + object + *not* + infinitive)
>
> Other verbs that follow this pattern:
> *advise   ask   persuade   remind   teach   want*

7 a) Rewrite these sentences so that they mean the same, using the verb in parentheses.

1 Doug said to me, "Be more careful." (*tell*)
  Doug told me to be more careful .

2 "Juliet, please stay," Jim said. (*want*)
  Jim ....

3 My father gave me driving lessons last year. (*teach*)
  My father ....

4 The local people said we shouldn't drink the water. (*advise*)
  The local people ....
  ....

5 "Sarah, could you get me some aspirin," John said. (*ask*)
  John ....

6 After a lot of discussion, the travel agent agreed to give Toni and Jo a discount. (*persuade*)
  Toni and Jo ....
  ....

7 "Don't forget to lock the back door," my mother told me. (*remind*)
  My mother ....

8 "Don't touch the computer," we said to the children. (*tell*)
  We ....

9 "I think you should go to the police," Ian said to Martin. (*advise*)
  Ian ....

10 "Please don't make so much noise," Todd said to his neighbor. (*ask*)
  Todd ....

b) Complete these sentences so that they are true for you.

1 If someone was visiting my city, I'd advise ....
  ....

2 It's not easy to persuade me ....
  ....

3 People always have to remind me ....
  ....

4 If I had a daughter, I'd want her ....
  ....

5 I sometimes ask my English teacher to ....
  ....

Jazz chant

Verbs that describe behavior and reactions

8 a) Read the jazz chant and complete the sentences with the best form of the verb in parentheses, adding a preposition if necessary.

Tom persuaded his mother (1) *to lend* (lend) him her car
And promised (2) .... (get) back by eight.
His mother agreed (3) .... (give) him the keys
And trusted him not to be late.
When the police brought him home at a quarter to two
She ran down the stairs from her bed.
"We suspect this young man (4) .... (tell) us lies."
She refused (5) .... (believe) what they said.
She insisted (6) .... (hear) his side of the tale.
He admitted (7) .... (drive) too fast
But strongly denied (8) .... (have) too much to drink:
"My first glass of beer was my last."
The officers threatened (9) .... (take) him away.
His mom wouldn't let them and she
Suggested (10) .... (discuss) the case the next day.
They did, and they let him go free.

b) 📼 Listen to the jazz chant and say it with the cassette.

Vocabulary

Using the dictionary: review

> **re·act** /ri'ækt/ v [I] **1** to behave in a particular way because of something that has happened or something that has been said to you: [**+ to**] *How did Wilson react to your idea?*
> **react against sth** *phr v* [T] to show that you dislike someone else's rules or way of doing something by deliberately doing the opposite: *Feminists reacted against women's traditional roles.*
>
> When you look a word up in the dictionary it shows you:
> • the pronunciation /ri'ækt/, including the main stress (shown by ')
> • the grammar, e.g. *v* = verb, *n* = noun
> • if a noun is countable [C] or uncountable [U]
> • if there is a preposition that follows it, e.g. **react** (**to**, **against**)
> • the meaning, and gives example sentences.

9 **a)** Use these extracts from the *Longman Dictionary of Contemporary English* to complete the chart below. Mark the main stress ●.

ad·vice /əd'vaɪs/ *n* [U] an opinion you give someone about what they should do: [**+ on/about**] *There's lots of advice in the book on baby care.* | **give advice** *Can you give me some advice about buying a house?*

ad·vi·sab·le /əd'vaɪzəbəl/ *adj* something that is advisable should be done in order to avoid problems: *For heavy smokers, regular medical checks are advisable.*

ad·vise /əd'vaɪz/ *v* to tell someone what you think they should do: **advise sb to do sth** *Passengers are advised not to leave their bags unattended.*

de·cide /dɪ'saɪd/ *v* to make a choice or judgment about something: **decide to do sth** *Tina's decided to go to Prague for her vacation.*

de·ci·sion /dɪ'sɪʒən/ *n* [C] a choice or judgment that you make after a period of discussion or thought: *The judge's decision is final.* | **make/take a decision** (=decide) *The committee will make its decision this week.*

de·ci·sive /dɪ'saɪsɪv/ *adj* good at making decisions quickly and with confidence: *a decisive leader*

ig·no·rance /'ɪgnərəns/ *n* [U] no knowledge or information about something: *My mistake was caused by ignorance.*

ig·no·rant /'ɪgnərənt/ *adj* not knowing facts or information that you ought to know: *an ignorant man* | [**+ about**] *I'm very ignorant about politics.*

ig·nore /ɪg'nɔːr/ *v* to behave as if you had not heard or seen someone or something: *Either she didn't see me or she deliberately ignored me.*

know[1] /noʊ/ *v past tense* knew / njuː/ *past participle* known /noʊn/ to have information about something: *Who knows the answer?*

knowl·edge /'nɑːlɪdʒ/ *n* [U] the facts, skills, and understanding that you have gained through learning or experience: [**+ of**] *His knowledge of ancient civilizations is wonderful.*

knowl·edge·a·ble /'nɑːlɪdʒəbəl/ *adj* knowing a lot: [**+ about**] *Graham's very knowledgeable about wines.*

so·lu·tion /sə'luːʃən/ *n* [C] a way of solving a problem or dealing with a difficult situation: [**+ to**] *There are no simple solutions to the problem of overpopulation.* **find a solution** *The governments are trying to find a peaceful solution.*

solve /sɑːlv/ *v* to find or provide a way of dealing with a problem: *Charlie thinks money will solve all his problems.*

verb	noun	adjective
advíse	advice	
decide		
ignore		
know		
	solution	–

b) Circle the correct answer in these sentences.

1 After "knowledge" we use the preposition ⟨of⟩ / *about*.

2 "Advice" is a *countable* / *uncountable* noun.

3 The pronunciation of "advice" and "advise" is *the same* / *different*.

4 In "ignore" the letter "g" is *silent* / *not silent*.

5 After "solution" we use the preposition *to* / *at*.

6 "Solution" is a *countable* / *uncountable* noun.

7 People *make* / *do* a decision.

8 The pronunciation of the first "i" in "decisive" and "decision" is the *same* / *different*.

c) Complete these sentences with the correct word (use the dictionary extracts).

1 It's not ..*advisable*.. to swim immediately after a big meal.

2 Pauline's very knowledgeable .... jazz music.

3 Have you .... a solution to your problem yet?

4 The teacher .... Jim's question and continued talking.

5 I'm not very .... when I go shopping: it takes me a long time to choose clothes.

6 Could you give my daughter .... advice about music lessons?

7 The teacher was shocked by the children's .... : they knew nothing about the history of their country.

8 The solution .... the problem isn't easy.

9 The journalist's .... of the political situation was very good.

Real life

Starting and finishing conversations

10 **a)** Match the speech bubbles to make complete phrases for starting and finishing conversations.

1 | I'm sorry to interrupt but I have to ...

a | ... getting here?

b | ... the time?

2 | It's getting ...

c | ... go now.

3 | Hello, I've heard ...

d | ... must rush.

4 | How are you? I haven't ...

e | ... in Prague.

5 | Hi, glad you ...

f | ... a lot about you.

6 | Did you have any problems ...

g | ... could come.

h | ... late.

7 | Oh dear, is that ...

i | ... seen you for ages.

8 | I really ...

9 | I hear you're going to study ...

1 ..*c*.. 2 .... 3 .... 4 .... 5 .... 6 ....

7 .... 8 .... 9 ....

b) Now write the complete phrases in the correct column in the chart.

Starting conversations	Finishing conversations
1 *Hello, I've heard a lot about you.*	6
2	7
3	8
4	9
5	

c) Look at the following situations, which take place at a party. Choose the best phrase (1–9 above) for each situation.

You're having a party. The doorbell rings, you open the door and see two good friends. What do you say?

Hi, glad you could come ....

2 It's a cold night and there's ice on the roads. You know they came by car. As you take their coats, what do you say?

....

3 As you go into the party, your friend Simon comes up and sees your guests. It's a long time since he has seen them. What does he say?

....

4 You take your friends into the party and introduce them to your sister. What does your sister say?

....

5 Later at the party, one of your guests introduces his girlfriend to you. You don't know very much about her, except that she's going to study in Prague. What do you say?

....

6 It's 11:30. You're in the middle of a conversation and a friend who lives a long way away comes up to you. What does he say?

....

7 It's one o'clock. You've been having a very interesting conversation with one of your guests when she suddenly looks at her watch. What does she say? (Two phrases together)

....

d) 🔲 Listen to the situations and say the correct phrase.

You hear:

You're having a party. The doorbell rings and you see two good friends.

You say:

Hi, glad you could come.

Improve your writing

A letter to sort out a problem

11 **a)** Lucy Humphries booked a flight to Mexico City and paid by credit card. She received her ticket a few days later, but the dates on the ticket were wrong. She sent the ticket back to the travel agent's, but nearly two weeks have passed and she has not heard from them.

Lucy has written a letter to sort out the problem. Reorder the sentences below and write out the complete letter in the space provided.

> A week later, I received my credit card receipt and the ticket, but unfortunately the dates were wrong.

> That was 10 days ago, and I have heard nothing from you since then.

> You booked me onto a flight costing £425, which I paid by credit card.

> I look forward to hearing from you.

> As you can imagine, I am very concerned about this because I need to make other arrangements for my trip, which I cannot do until the dates are confirmed.

> Several weeks ago I telephoned your office to book a round-trip flight to Mexico City, leaving on July 8 and returning on July 27.

> I would therefore be grateful if you could look into this matter immediately.

> I immediately returned the ticket by registered mail, with a note explaining the problem.

```
                                    44 Barn Road
                                    Nottingham NS4
                                    May 29, 2004

The Manager
Eurotrips Travel Agent's

Dear Sir/Madam,

.................................................
.................................................
.................................................
.................................................
.................................................
.................................................
.................................................
.................................................
.................................................
.................................................
.................................................
.................................................
.................................................
.................................................
.................................................
.................................................
.................................................

Sincerely,

L. Humphries
```

b) In your notebook write a letter to sort out the problem below.
Use the letter above to help you and show your letter to your teacher.

> Three weeks ago, you booked a 4-week course at the Success Language School, 354 Liffey Road, Dublin DN6. A week ago, you had not received a receipt or confirmation of your place on the course. You phoned the school and left a message on the answering machine, but you have still not heard anything.
>
> Before you write the letter, decide:
> • How many hours a day your course is: 3 / 4 / 5 ?
> • How you paid for the course: credit card / bank transfer?
> • The dates of your course.